CONVEYANCING 2001

CONVEYANCING 2001

KENNETH G. C. REID WS

Professor of Property Law in the University of Edinburgh

and

GEORGE L. GRETTON WS

Lord President Reid Professor of Law in the University of Edinburgh

Butterworths
LexisNexis™

Members of the LexisNexis Group worldwide

United Kingdom	LexisNexis Butterworths Tolley, a Division of Reed Elsevier (UK) Ltd, 4 Hill Street, EDINBURGH EH2 3JZ and Halsbury House, 35 Chancery Lane, LONDON WC2A 1EL
Argentina	LexisNexis Argentina, BUENOS AIRES
Australia	LexisNexis Butterworths, CHATSWOOD, New South Wales
Austria	LexisNexis Verlag ARD Orac GmbH & Co KG, VIENNA
Canada	LexisNexis Butterworths, MARKHAM, Ontario
Chile	LexisNexis Chile Ltda, SANTIAGO DE CHILE
Czech Republic	Nakladatelství Orac sro, PRAGUE
France	Editions du Juris-Classeur SA, PARIS
Hong Kong	LexisNexis Butterworths, HONG KONG
Hungary	HVG-Orac, BUDAPEST
India	LexisNexis Butterworths, NEW DELHI
Ireland	Butterworths (Ireland) Ltd, DUBLIN
Italy	Giuffré Editore, MILAN
Malaysia	Malayan Law Journal Sdn Bhd, KUALA LUMPUR
New Zealand	Butterworths of New Zealand, WELLINGTON
Poland	Wydawnictwa Prawnicze LexisNexis, WARSAW
Singapore	LexisNexis Butterworths, SINGAPORE
South Africa	Butterworths SA, DURBAN
Switzerland	Stämpfli Verlag AG, BERNE
USA	LexisNexis, DAYTON, Ohio

A CIP Catalogue record for this book is available from the British Library.

ISBN 0 406 95703 7

Typeset by Waverley Typesetters, Galashiels
Printed and bound in Great Britain by Hobbs The Printers Ltd, Totton, Hampshire

Visit Butterworths LexisNexis *direct* at : www.butterworthsscotland.com

CONTENTS

PART II : STATUTORY DEVELOPMENTS

PART III : OTHER MATERIAL

PART IV : COMMENTARY

PART V : TABLES

PREFACE

This volume surveys the developments in conveyancing law and practice during calendar year 2001. It is divided into five parts. There is, first, a brief description of all cases reported in 2001 (as well as a few decided in that year but not yet reported). The next two parts summarise, respectively, statutory developments during 2001 and other material of interest to conveyancers. The fourth part is a detailed commentary on selected issues arising from the first three parts. Finally, in part V, there are two tables. The first, a cumulative table of appeals, is designed to facilitate moving from one annual volume to the next. The second is a table of cases digested in *Conveyancing 2000* but reported, either for the first time or in an additional series, in 2001. This is for convenience of future reference.

We do not seek to cover agricultural holdings, crofting, public sector tenancies (except the right-to-buy legislation), compulsory purchase or planning law. Otherwise our coverage is intended to be complete. But we should say that this book, being carried through quickly, cannot have all the qualities to be expected of a work prepared at leisure.

We are grateful to Professor Roddy Paisley of the University of Aberdeen for providing us with the pleadings and opinions in a number of cases from the sheriff court. We are also indebted to Mr Alan Barr and Dr Andrew Steven, both of the University of Edinburgh, and to Mr Scott Wortley of the University of Strathclyde, for help of various kinds.

Kenneth G C Reid
George L Gretton
10 February 2002

TABLE OF CASES

TABLE OF STATUTES

TABLE OF STATUTORY INSTRUMENTS

PART I

CASES

Note that the full text of all decisions of the Court of Session is available on the Scottish Courts website (www.scotcourts.gov.uk/).

MISSIVES

(1) Adams v Young 2001 GWD 3–127 (OH)

The pursuer purchased 5 Grange Loan, Edinburgh in 1995. This was a former shop which had been converted into a house by the defenders. It was represented by the defenders (it was averred), both orally and in the sale particulars, that the flat had enjoyed full renovation and improvement. Three years later a secret room was discovered, extending to some 80 square feet. This was half full of waste and building materials and was said to have been the source of an outbreak of dry rot. The pursuer sought damages on the basis of fraudulent misrepresentation. He claimed both for (i) an overpayment of £7,000 (on the basis the flat with the secret room was worth less than the flat without it) and (ii) the cost of subsequent remedial works. Proof before answer allowed in respect of (i). In respect of (ii) the pursuer had already disponed the flat to his sister, gratuitously, before the room was discovered, and so no loss had been incurred by the pursuer. (In fact, although the disposition was granted and presented for recording before discovery of the room, it was not recorded until after the discovery; but nothing was made of this point.) See **Commentary** p 64.

(2) Barry v Sutherland 2001 GWD 38–1431 (OH)

Missives of sale were concluded in respect of the Waterfront Bar, Wick. The purchasers were to lease for a year and then acquire ownership. Missives were entered into in reliance on trading accounts which (it was averred) inflated the net profit by getting on for 100%. The purchasers sued for damages for fraud. In cases like this the purchasers usually seek the amount by which they have overpaid (as in the previous case). But this could not be done here because, an escape clause having been invoked, the purchase was not now to proceed. A further difficulty was that the most direct loss had been incurred, not by the purchasers, but by a company which they owned and which had suffered a trading loss in operating the bar. The purchasers' loss was that they had advanced money to the company, which money was now irrecoverable. The seller challenged whether such a loss could be claimed for. **Held**: Proof before answer allowed. Lord Eassie's view was that if the purchasers were induced by fraudulent misrepresentations 'to embark on the commercial venture of exploiting the Waterfront Bar to their financial detriment' they 'are entitled to recover the financial loss to them which directly flows from their having embarked on that course'.

[A related case is digested at (55).]

(3) Argus Care Ltd v Balmoral Nursing Homes Ltd
2001 GWD 29–1155 (Sh Ct)

This was a dispute as to whether sellers of a nursing home had failed to comply with certain warranties in the missives, and in particular a warranty that the business was carried out in accordance with health board regulations. The argument turned on the staffing levels required by the Nursing Homes Registration (Scotland) Regulations 1990. The purchasers claimed negligent misrepresentation and sought damages in respect of an alleged overpayment for the property. **Held**: Action dismissed. The sellers' interpretation of the Regulations was not negligent. And the purchasers' pleadings were unsatisfactory in a number of respects.

(4) Cole v Lonie 2001 SC 610, 2001 SLT 608, 2001 SCLR 717 (IH)

Missives of let were concluded on 1 December 1982 in relation to the basement at 5–7 Old Fishmarket Close, Edinburgh. A formal lease followed. The basement was to be used as a restaurant, and the rest of the tenement for residential purposes. The missives provided that:

> Your clients [ie the lessor] will be solely responsible for the expense of bringing the kitchen ventilation system up to standard including any additional works required in connection with the conversion of the premises above the residential purposes. Your clients will also be responsible for the expense of separating the subjects of lease from the remainder of the tenement.

In 1990 investigations by the lessee uncovered defects in the ventilation system. In 1992 further investigations revealed that there was insufficient separation of the restaurant from the flat above. The lessee sought damages in respect of the latter. The action was raised in 1997, within five years of the discovery of the specific defect but more than five years after the initial discoveries of 1990. It was accepted that the relevant prescriptive period was five years and not 20 years (as it would have been for those clauses of the missives which could be characterised as obligations relating to land). But as respects obligations to make 'reparation', the five-year prescription does not run (in a case where the claimant was unaware of the injury) until he was so aware or could with reasonable diligence have become so aware. (See s 11(3) of the Prescription and Limitation (Scotland) Act 1973.) The question then became when the lessor became, or could have become, aware that the separation was incomplete. Was it in 1990, when the first investigations were made, or in 1992? If 1990 were correct, the claim would fail. **Held**: The relevant clause in the missives created two distinct obligations, in relation respectively to ventilation and separation. The 1990 investigation concerned only the first of those. Hence the lessee's knowledge of the default in relation to the second dated only from 1992. So the claim had not prescribed.

Two other matters may be mentioned, though they do not appear to have been argued. (1) The missives were expressly stated to be of a continuing nature, notwithstanding entry. As the law stood in 1982 this may not have been sufficient to prevent the missives from being superseded by the formal lease. (2) The obligation on the lessor was, it seems, not to carry out works but merely to pay for them. Yet the action was for damages for breach and not for payment in implement. The nature of the supposed breach is unclear.

(5) Morston Assets Ltd v City of Edinburgh Council 2001 SLT 613 (OH)

Edinburgh Council put some land on the market. The pursuers put in an offer after the closing date. (An earlier offer had not been accepted.) Although this was the highest, it was not accepted, on the basis that it was too late. The pursuers sought judicial review. Their argument was that the Council had a statutory obligation, under s 74 of the Local Government (Scotland) Act 1973, to obtain the best price that can reasonably be obtained for land sold, and that their offer constituted the best price. **Held**: Petition dismissed. No doubt as a matter of strict law the Council could have accepted a late offer. But such a practice was not well-regarded, and might have prejudiced future sales by the Council. Accordingly, in accepting a lower offer the Council had achieved the best price reasonably obtainable within s 74.

(6) Glasgow City Council v Caststop Ltd 2002 SLT 47 (OH)

Clawback. Missives provided for the payment of additional sums 'in the event that the purchaser achieves planning permission for the erection or re-development of the subjects for more than forty-nine residential units'. The planning permission originally granted was indeed for 49 units, but three months later the planning permission was varied to allow 61 units. The second application, however, was not by the purchasers but by a wholly-owned subsidiary which had just been formed. Later, some of the land was actually transferred to the subsidiary. When the sellers sought to invoke the clawback, the purchasers argued that planning permission had been 'achieved' not by them but by their subsidiary. The clause in missives did not merely require that planning permission be granted. It required that it be achieved by the purchasers. In the present case it had not been so achieved. **Held**: The clause did not require that the application actually be made by the purchasers. Rather they had to 'achieve' it. No doubt if the application had been by some remote third party, no credit for the achievement could be given to the purchasers. But here there was direct involvement at least to the extent that the purchasers had formed the subsidiary. Hence, as a matter of reasonable construction, they could be said to have 'achieved' planning permission for 61 units. The additional sums were accordingly due.

The case contains citation and discussion of a number of leading modern cases, mainly from England. In reaching his view Lord Macfadyen took account not only of the words used but of the surrounding circumstances and of the need to reach a result which was commercially sensible. But in the event the words were paramount.

If they had lost on the interpretation point, the sellers had intended to seek to prove that the subsidiary company applied for planning permission as agents of the purchasers.

(7) Bryant Homes (Scotland) Ltd v Secretary of State for Scotland 2001 GWD 19–738 (IH)

This was a stated case from an arbiter. Fact-specific case on interpretation of terms such as 'exceptional costs'. The arbiter's findings were approved.

(8) Albatown Ltd v Credential Group Ltd 2001 GWD 27–1102 (OH)

Credential Group Ltd owned 21 Watson Street, Glasgow. They sold to Federal Securities Ltd. The disposition narrated that the price was paid in full, but in fact only part of it was paid. The buyers granted to the sellers a standard security over the property, in security of 'our whole obligations to Credential Group Ltd . . . by virtue of the missives between us . . .' A copy of the missives was annexed and signed as relative to the standard security. The missives were superseded after two years, but by that time the balance of the price remained unpaid. The pursuers, who were successors in title of Federal Securities Ltd, sought declarator 'that the obligations secured by the standard security . . . were extinguished' on the expiry of the two-year period. **Held**: that, since the balance of the price was due only in terms of the missives, the supersession of the missives meant that the balance of the price was no longer payable, and hence the standard security no longer secured anything. See **Commentary** pp 63 and 91.

[Other aspects of this case are digested at (63).]

OPTIONS

(9) Spence v Murray (Alford) Ltd 2001 GWD 7–265 (Sh Ct)

An option to purchase, constituted by missives, was exercised on 28 January 1984. In terms of the missives the date of entry was to be 40 days later (10 April 1984). The transaction does not seem to have progressed any further. Much later, the purchaser raised an action for implement. The defence was a clause in the missives that the missives 'would cease to be enforceable after a period of two years from the date of entry except insofar as they are founded upon in any court proceedings which have commenced within the said period'. The purchaser argued that this must be read as meaning two years after delivery of the disposition, an event yet to occur. **Held**: The clause clearly meant two years after the stipulated date of entry (10 April 1984). Hence, the option had ceased to be enforceable.

(10) Bogie v Forestry Commission 2001 GWD 38–1432 (OH)

Bogie negotiated with the Forestry Commission for them to grant him an option to buy certain land, and the parties then instructed solicitors to prepare a formal agreement. Before this could be done, the sellers decided not to proceed. The purchaser argued that the effect of the negotiations was to create a concluded contract. Hence, the sellers could not withdraw. **Held**: In an option, as in an ordinary contract of sale, there must be agreement as to parties, price and property. In the present case the negotiations did not disclose agreement as to either price or property. See **Commentary** p 61.

BOUNDARY WALLS AND GABLES

(11) Powrie Castle Properties Ltd v Dundee City Council
2001 SCLR 146 (Sh Ct)

Two adjoining tenements were separated by a mutual gable. The defenders, owners of one, demolished their building, employing independent contractors. As a result, the gable was exposed to the weather and water penetrated into the remaining building, owned by the pursuers. When the defenders failed to carry out further repairs, the pursuers did the necessary work and sought to recover the cost. Their claim was based on nuisance. **Held**: Proof allowed.

SERVITUDES AND RIGHTS OF WAY

(12) Davidson v Wiseman 2001 GWD 9–317 (Sh Ct)

Circumstances in which there was insufficient evidence of possession for a servitude of way to be established by prescription. Had such a servitude been established it might have included a right to park cars. See **Commentary** p 72.

(13) Moss Bros Group plc v Scottish Mutual Assurance plc
2001 SC 779, 2001 SLT 641 (OH)

A minute of agreement between two neighbouring owners granted mutual rights of egress for fire escape purposes. Circumstances in which the rights were held to be servitudes binding successors. See **Commentary** p 74.

(14) Soriani v Cluckie 2001 GWD 28–1138 (Sh Ct)

A dispute between neighbours. Property A had a servitude of access over a pend leading to property B. Property B had a servitude of access over a yard at the rear of property A. The pend had gates but the practice had been to keep them open during business hours. The owner of property A was granted interdict to prevent the owner of property B (i) locking the gates during business hours and (ii) using the yard (over which he had a servitude) for the exercise of his two dogs. On (ii) see **Commentary** p 73.

(15) McKellar v Aberdeen City Council
2001 SC 729, 2001 SLT 662 (OH)

Aberdeen Council placed 20 substantial wheelie bins at various points at the side of the road in Wallfield Crescent. Each was 4 feet 8 inches × 4 feet 2 inches × 3 feet 3 inches. The bins were for domestic refuse for the tenements in the street, and prevented seagulls from attacking the bags. Mr McKellar, who lived in the street, was unhappy with the new bins and sought judicial review of the Council's decision. The Council argued (i) that the bins narrowed the street and so could be regarded as a form of traffic calming, which was permitted by s 39A of the Roads (Scotland) Act 1984, or alternatively (ii) that the bins were 'for the collection and temporary deposit of road refuse' within s 54 of the Act. **Held**: Neither ground justified the placing of the bins, and the decision complained about fell to be reduced. In relation to (i) Lord MacLean expressed scepticism as to the traffic calming value of structures which were parked in spaces normally used for cars and which took up no more room. And in relation to (ii), he decided that 'road refuse' meant refuse by users of the road and not ordinary domestic refuse.

(16) Labinski Ltd v BP Oil Development Ltd 2002 GWD 1–46 (OH)

Predecessors of the pursuers granted a servitude for a pipeline to BP. This positive servitude was reinforced by a negative servitude prohibiting building works within 10 feet of either side of the pipe. One of the conditions of the servitudes was that:

> If at any time the Owner wishes to develop land affected by the pipeline, or to accept an offer from some person who wishes to develop such land, the Owner shall if the said proposed development of the land is prevented in whole or in part by reason only of the existence of the pipeline, give written notice to the Company of the said proposed development including details of the application for and refusal of or conditional grant of planning permission in principle by the Planning Authority. Within six calendar months of the receipt of such written notice, the Company shall give their decision in writing to the Owner that they intend to divert the pipeline or that they intend to pay compensation for all losses arising from their decision not to divert the pipeline, including, without prejudice to the foregoing generality, losses of Development Value.

The pursuers, having been refused planning permission for a development, claimed £31 million from BP. **Held**: Action dismissed. The existence of the pipeline was only one of the reasons for the refusal of planning permission.

Doubt has sometimes been expressed as to whether a pipeline servitude is one of the known servitudes and hence competent in Scots law, and also as to whether, even if competent, such a servitude can be created in the absence of a proper dominant tenement. In this litigation, however, the validity of the servitude was taken for granted. Any doubts as to the competency of pipeline servitudes will be removed (as and when enacted) by s 73 of the Title Conditions (Scotland) Bill, the terms of which are retrospective.

BP were the original holders of the servitude right. It is open to question as to whether an obligation to pay compensation would be binding on their successors. To bind successors a servitude condition must be praedial, ie must relate to the two properties. See D J Cusine and R R M Paisley, *Servitudes and Rights of Way* (1998) para 14.08.

REAL BURDENS

(17) Grampian Joint Police Board v Pearson
2001 SC 772, 2001 SLT 734 (IH)

Land was feued in 1901 for the erection of a police house. The feu charter provided that, if the house was sold for private use, the superiors would be entitled to buy it back at a price not greater than 'the original cost of said buildings'. **Held**: Since that cost could only be ascertained, if at all, with great difficulty and with the use of extensive extrinsic evidence, the obligation could not be said to be contained within the four corners of the deed and so could not be a valid real burden. See **Commentary** p 88.

[This affirms the decision of the Lord Ordinary reported at 2001 SLT 90 (*Conveyancing 2000* Case (18) and p 74).]

(18) Hampden Park Ltd v Dow 2001 SCLR 951, 2002 SLT 95 (OH)

As well as operating the National Stadium (ie Hampden) the pursuers were also local superiors. In particular they were superiors in relation to premises at 37 Carmunnock Road and 6 Letherby Drive. Letherby Drive is a private road leading to Hampden. One of the burdens in the title provided that:

> The second party and his foresaids shall be bound to leave open and free of buildings or other obstructions so far as forming part of the plots of ground hereby disponed ... Letherby Drive ...

The premises in question were leased out, and since November 1999 the lessees had cut the width of the road to a half, first by parking a car at right angles into the road and thereafter by erecting a barrier. The effect was to prevent the road from being used by large vehicles such as coaches and ambulances. In those circumstances the pursuers sought interdict from placing or maintaining in place, or from causing or permitting any other persons to put or maintain in place any obstructions including without prejudice to the generality any bollards, fences, posts, gates, cones, signs, sleeping policemen or other traffic calming or inhibiting devices, in, on or near the section of the carriageway of Letherby Drive . . .

Interim interdict having been granted, the defenders sought recall. No defence was offered on the merits but it was argued that interdict could not be used where, as here, the remedy being sought was in essence positive in nature (ie required the defenders to remove the fence). **Held**: The circumstances in which interdict could be used were authoritatively considered in *Church Commissioners for England* v *Abbey National plc* 1994 SC 651, 1994 SLT 959. 'If the court's order is in substance wholly negative, and there is no need to specify any positive action to be taken by the defender for the order to be effective, the fact that positive actings will in fact be required to comply with the order is not a bar to interdict. If, on the other hand, the pursuer requires to specify in the order sought precisely what positive actings the defender must take to comply, interdict is incompetent' (2002 SLT 95, 99J–K). The order sought in the present case fell within the first of these situations. Hence interdict was competent.

In the past there has been some controversy as to whether a real burden can be enforced against a person who is not owner of the burdened property, but it is now generally accepted that negative obligations, at least, may be enforced against tenants and other occupiers. This case is another example of such a remedy being granted.

(19) Morrison v Lindsay
Glasgow Sheriff Court, 4 October 2001, case no 2234/01 (unreported)

A deed of conditions contained a prohibition on using the property for any trade or profession without the written consent of the superiors. Neighbours were given express enforcement rights under the deed. The defender obtained the superiors' consent to use the property for child-minding. Nonetheless it was **held** that a neighbour still had title to insist on the prohibition. See **Commentary** p 89.

A subsidiary issue which was raised but not decided was whether enforcement in the courts was competent in the face of a clause providing for compulsory arbitration.

(20) Graham & Sibbald v Brash
Dundee Sheriff Court, 21 March 2001 (unreported)

A deed of conditions in a substantial residential development contained an obligation 'to maintain in good order and repair and when necessary renew the common amenity areas'. The common amenity areas included a swimming pool. When the defender, owner of one of the houses of the development, refused to contribute to the running costs of the pool, an action for payment was raised by the pursuers, who managed the development. **Held**: Real burdens are to be interpreted strictly and in favour of freedom, and on that basis an obligation to maintain did not include an obligation to pay for running costs. Hence the defender was not liable. See **Commentary** p 85.

(21) Hanover (Scotland) Housing Association Ltd Ptr
2002 SCLR 144

This litigation is the culmination of a long-running and bitter dispute at Millbrae Gardens, Glasgow (a sheltered/retirement housing development) between the superiors, Hanover Housing, and the owners of a number of the flats. When the dispute went to arbitration in 1996 the arbiter directed that the deed of conditions should be altered in a number of respects so as to give management power to a majority of owners rather than, as at present, to Hanover. Hanover challenged these findings. One ground of challenge was that the deed of conditions could not competently be altered. Unusually, the deed had a provision on the subject:

> The superiors shall have the right to waive or vary any or all of the said burdens and others with the consent of a majority of those voting at a meeting of the property council called for that purpose . . .

Nonetheless, it was argued for Hanover (i) that variation did not include the creation of *new* real burdens and (ii) that in any event it would be contrary to principle for variation by a bare majority to have the effect of making an existing burden more onerous for the minority. The argument is not without merit. Certainly the general rule is that variation requires the consent of all of the burdened owners and not merely of some lesser percentage. The same is true for the creation of new burdens. What is unclear is whether that general rule can be altered in the deed of conditions. In the event Lord Wheatley was persuaded that the proposed alterations were genuine and (from the point of view of other owners at least) innocuous and so fell within the clause. Hence there was no difficulty in altering the deed of conditions in the manner ordered by the arbiter, and this should now be done by Hanover without delay.

The uncertainty in the common law will be removed by the Title Conditions (Scotland) Bill (as and when enacted). The device of making provision in a deed of conditions for variation by a majority or other percentage of owners is expressly recognised (ss 30(2)(a) and 31(2)(a)); and 'variation' is defined (s 113(1)) as including the imposition of a new burden.

VARIATION AND DISCHARGE OF LAND OBLIGATIONS

(22) Sportstune Motor Co Ltd v Sarwar 2001 GWD 7–259 (Lands Tr)

In 1978 a filling station was separated from an adjacent garage business. The applicants bought the filling station. In the disposition a servitude of vehicular access was reserved over the forecourt. This was the main means of access to the garage. Subsequently, the garage closed, the site was used for other purposes, and other means of vehicular access were acquired. Later the filling station also closed, and the existence of the servitude was now proving an impediment to development of the site. When the owners sought discharge of the servitude this was opposed by the owner of the former garage. **Held**: Discharge granted under s 1(3)(a) of the 1970 Act (obligation unreasonable due to changes in land or neighbourhood). Both sites had changed, and the access was no longer necessary for the former garage.

(23) Scott v Robinson 2001 GWD 7–261 (Lands Tr)

The Lands Tribunal dischared a pedestrian servitude of way under s 1(3)(a) of the 1970 Act. The servitude was originally designed for a business on the dominant tenement which had now closed. An alternative access had since come into existence. This could be used for the wheelie bin which, so the dominant proprietor argued, was better suited to the servitude access.

(24) Henderson v Barden 2001 Hous LR 113 (Lands Tr)

This case concerned three terraced houses, numbers 2, 4 and 6 Murrayshall Road, Scone. Access to the main road from the front of numbers 4 and 6 was by means of a path through number 2. For this there was a properly constituted servitude. The path passed near the house. The owner of number 2 sought a variation of the servitude to the effect of re-routing it so that it was at the other end of the garden. This was opposed by the owners of numbers 4 and 6. From their point of view the re-routing had a number of disadvantages. The proposed new route was longer and less direct. The garden at that point was a metre higher than the road so that steps or excavation would be necessary. And in order to reach the new entrance to number 2 from number 4 it would be necessary to make a new path diagonally across the garden in number 4. As against this, the re-routing had the advantage for the owner of number 2 that the path would be far less intrusive. She argued her case on the basis of paras (a) and (b) of s 1(3) of the Conveyancing and Feudal Reform (Scotland) Act 1970. (Para (c), usually the most promising ground, was not available because the servitude did not impede a use). **Held**: Application refused. The only change in the character of the neighbourhood put forward under para (a) was the creation of alternative accesses from the rear of numbers 4 and 6 to a different road. But a kitchen access is not the same as an access through the front door. Thus, it could not be said that the continued existence of the servitude was now 'unreasonable or inappropriate'. The case also failed under para (b) (obligation unduly burdensome compared with any benefit). This was not a case where there was minimal benefit. The present route of the path conferred obvious benefits which would be lost if it were to be re-routed in the manner suggested.

It might be added that a Lands Tribunal application is not always necessary for re-routing. In certain cases this can be done unilaterally by the owner of the servient tenement. But the balance of modern authority is to the effect that this is not possible where, as here, the route of the servitude is laid down in the original deed. See D J Cusine and R R M Paisley, *Servitudes and Rights of Way* (1998) para 12.43.

(25) Itelsor v Smith 2001 Hous LR 120 (Lands Tr)

12 Harefield Road, Dundee. A disposition of 1924 restricted development to a single house. In an opposed application the restriction was discharged to the extent of allowing a development of four houses and two flats, for which planning permission had been obtained. The ground of discharge was s 1(3)(c) of the 1970 Act (existence of the obligation impeding some reasonable use of the land). The case contains a helpful analysis of the role of planning permission, and of the proper method of assessing the reasonableness of a proposed use. See **Commentary** p 101.

(26) Moran's Exrs v Shenstone Properties Ltd
2001 Hous LR 124 (Lands Tr)

67 Coillesdene Avenue, Edinburgh. Part of the site was sold for the construction of a second house. A second house was contrary to a feuing condition imposed in 1936. The superiors' price for a waiver was £7,500. The superiors did not own any land in the neighbourhood. The Tribunal discharged the burden under both s 1(3)(b) and 1(3)(c) of the 1970 Act. A claim by the superiors for compensation was refused. See **Commentary** p 99.

(27) Strathclyde Joint Police Board v The Elderslie Estates Ltd
2002 SLT (Lands Tr) 2

A feu contract of a building plot, in 1942, restricted its use to that of a police station and police house. Now it was surplus to police requirements. Negotiations broke down over the cost of a waiver. The Police Board were willing to pay £1000 but the superiors wanted £10,000. When the Police Board applied to the Lands Tribunal for discharge the superiors did not oppose the application on the merits but argued for compensation, on the basis of s 1(4)(i) of the Conveyancing and Feudal Reform (Scotland) Act 1970 ('a sum to compensate for any substantial loss or disadvantage suffered by the proprietor as such benefited proprietor'). Since the superiors did not (it seems) own any neighbouring property, their loss was solely of the chance to exact payment for a waiver. Previous Lands Tribunal practice had been to refuse to award compensation on that ground, but the superiors argued that, standing the European Convention on Human Rights, this interpretation of s 1(4)(i) could no longer stand. **Held**: The previous interpretation was fully compatible with the ECHR and would not be departed from. The burden was discharged without compensation (other than £1000 by concession of the Police Board). See **Commentary** p 101.

[The ECHR aspects of this case are digested more fully at (83).]

PROPERTY ENQUIRY CERTIFICATES

(28) Anderson v Perth and Kinross Council 2000 SCLR 987 (Sh Ct)

Perth and Kinross Council issued a letter to the solicitors selling a property stating (i) that there was outline planning consent for three houses on the property and (ii) that the property was in an area zoned for residential use. This letter was duly exhibited to the purchasers' agents, and subsequently missives were concluded. The outline planning permission expired four weeks after entry but the purchasers took no steps to extend it, in reliance on (ii). Their initial plan was to develop an environmental centre, but to fall back on residential development if the centre did not prove viable. In the event they came to pursue the residential option and applied for planning permission. This was refused on the basis that, contrary to the council's letter, the subjects were in an area zoned for industrial use. The purchasers sued the council for damages. The main head of claim was the difference between the value of the property as a residential site and its (lower) value as an industrial site. At first instance the sheriff decided that, while the council had a duty to the purchasers and had been negligent, the loss arose, not from the council's letter, but from the purchasers' own failure to renew the planning consent. On appeal the sheriff principal **held** that, although the letter may not have been the sole cause of the loss, it was a substantial cause. Damages were awarded in respect of the decline in value of the property.

REGISTRATION OF TITLE

(29) Wilson v Inverclyde Council 2001 GWD 3–129 (OH)

This was successor litigation to *Wilson v Keeper of the Registers of Scotland* 2000 SLT 267 (for which see *Conveyancing 1999* pp 14 and 67). The dispute concerned Greenock Harbour which, since 1987, had been owned by Scottish Enterprise (formerly the Scottish Development Agency) on a title registered in the Land Register. The precise arguments of the pursuers are difficult to follow, but in essence it seemed to have been argued that (i) part or all of the Harbour was formerly owned by the Magistrates of Greenock; (ii) the principal conveyance to the Magistrates, in 1772, had the effect of creating a trust; (iii) in terms of the trust the property was inalienable; (iv) accordingly when the property was eventually conveyed away, in 1965, the conveyance was void; (v) the effect of the void conveyance was to make the Register inaccurate insofar as it showed Scottish Enterprise (the successors of the 1965 acquirers) as owner; (vi) Inverclyde Council were the successors of the Magistrates of Greenock and hence the trustees under the 1772 trust, and; (vii) the pursuers, as residents of Inverclyde, were beneficiaries under the trust.

The first litigation sought rectification of the Register. The Register, it was argued, was inaccurate. The 'true' owners were Inverclyde Council and not Scottish Enterprise, and so, the argument ran, the name of the former should be substituted for that of the latter. That action failed for a number of reasons. The pursuers failed to establish that the Register was inaccurate. But even if it was inaccurate Scottish Enterprise were proprietors in possession and there were no grounds for rectification. Furthermore, rectification could only be pursued by the trustees under the alleged trust (Inverclyde Council) and not by the beneficiaries.

In this latest action the pursuers sought to meet these difficulties by seeking an order that Inverclyde Council apply for rectification, or lend their name to an action by the pursuers for such rectification. The action failed. The court was not persuaded that the 1772 deed created a trust. Even if it did, it was not competent for beneficiaries to require a particular course of action of trustees where this was a matter within the trustees' discretion. And there was nothing in the pleadings to support the idea that rectification would in any event be granted.

(30) Tesco Stores Ltd v Keeper of the Registers of Scotland 2001 SLT (Lands Tr) 23

The same area of property was entered in two different title plans. Indemnity was excluded in one but not in the other. The proprietors under the title in which indemnity was excluded sought to rectify the Register against the proprietors under the other title, to the effect of removing the property from their title. The main defence offered was that they were proprietors in possession. **Held**: The defenders were not in possession, and rectification allowed.

This is an important decision raising a number of fundamental issues about registration of title. See **Commentary** p 108.

RIGHT-TO-BUY LEGISLATION

(31) Nicol v Shetland Islands Council 2001 GWD 7–274 (Lands Tr)

The landlords failed to respond timeously to an application to purchase, so the tenant applied to the Lands Tribunal under s 71 of the Housing (Scotland) Act 1987. The Tribunal agreed to issue an offer to sell on behalf of the landlords, and the case turned on the terms of the offer. It appears that the parties were at loggerheads over a whole range of matters. One matter on which the tenant was successful was in having an express provision as to access rights inserted in the offer. Much of the case turned on the question of the quality of the landlord's title, and here the tenant's arguments were rejected.

(32) Smith v Aberdeen City Council 2001 Hous LR 17 and 93 (Lands Tr)

A tenant applied to purchase and the landlords responded timeously with an offer to sell. But soon thereafter they withdrew their offer, before it had been accepted, on the ground that the property was not the tenant's principal residence. However, they failed to serve, within the one month period laid down by s 68 of the 1987 Act, a notice of refusal. When the tenant applied to the Tribunal, it was held, first, that a landlord can withdraw an offer to sell, but, following *East of Scotland Water Authority* v *Livingstone* 1999 SLT 869, that the landlords could no longer assert their objection. Whilst the Tribunal was bound by the *East of Scotland* case, it is worth noting that Lord President Rodger dissented in that decision, and the reasons for his dissent are powerful. One cannot help wondering whether *East of Scotland* might not one day be overruled.

(33) Smith v Dundee City Council 2001 Hous LR 78 (Lands Tr)

This was an application by a school janitor. The main question was whether he was bound to occupy the property for the better performance of his duties, in which case the right to buy would be excluded. What had happened was that janitors were no longer tied to specific schools but looked after 'clusters' of schools (and the janitors re-named 'facilities co-ordinators'). **Held**: that he was not bound to occupy the property for the better performance of his duties.

LEASES

(34) Ali v Khosla 2001 SCLR 1072 (IH)

Although an agricultural case (and hence normally outwith the scope of our survey), this raises general issues about constitution of leases. Backhill Croft of Overbrae, Turiff, was owned by Mr and Mrs Sarv Khosla. They lived in England but intended that their son should, when older, farm the land. In the meantime they agreed with the pursuer, Aslam Ali, that he could use the land. There was nothing in writing. Some years later the parties fell out, and the question for the court was whether Ali held a lease or not. If he did, then the provisions of the Agricultural Holdings (Scotland) Act 1991 would apply. Over the years Ali's occupation had varied, at some periods being as little as one tenth of the total acreage. Likewise his payments to the Khoslas had varied. The Sheriff at Banff took the view there was 'simply an understanding that he would contribute a reasonable sum, depending on the amount he made from use of the . . . fields'. Given no agreement as to either rent or subjects, there was no lease. The Sheriff's decision was upheld by the Extra Division.

(35) Miller v Clerical Medical Investment Group Ltd
2001 SCLR 990 (OH)

The pursuer was the tenant of a unit in the Princes Square Shopping Centre in Glasgow's Buchanan Street. She traded as a jeweller. The owners of the Centre, Clerical Medical Investment Group Ltd, allowed someone else to set up a jewellery kiosk in the mall. The pursuer raised an action of interdict against the landlords. She had three main arguments.

The first was that the kiosk was in the circulation area of the Centre, to which all tenants had certain rights. This argument failed since the rights to the circulation area were merely rights to enable tenants, shoppers and so on free access to the various parts of the Centre, and this small kiosk did not impede such access to any material extent.

The second argument was that in every lease there is an obligation on the landlord, implied by law, not to 'derogate from the grant'. By allowing competition from the kiosk, the landlord was causing commercial injury to the pursuer, and thus derogating from the original grant. Now, what are known as 'exclusivity' clauses are common in retail leases, whereby landlords bind themselves not to permit competition in neighbouring properties. Thus, in this case the pursuer was arguing that an exclusivity clause is implied by law. The Lord Ordinary had no hesitation in rejecting this argument, for the simple reason that the issue had long ago been settled by a Whole Court decision, *Craig* v *Miller* (1888) 15 R 1005. The pursuer's attempts to seek assistance from English authorities cut no ice.

The third argument for the pursuer was based on a clause in her lease which bound her 'not to carry on, use or permit the Premises to be used . . . (without the Landlord's prior consent) for any trade or business already or for the time being established in the Centre . . .' This argument also failed. This clause would not even have stopped the pursuer from competing with her neighbours, if the landlord so consented.

This was an action that was destined to fail. It does, however, point up the importance of exclusivity clauses for the commercial interests of tenants in shopping centres. On the difficult question of whether an exclusivity clause binds a singular successor of the landlord, see *Optical Express (Gyle) Ltd* v *Marks & Spencer plc* 2000 SLT 644, discussed in *Conveyancing* 2000 pp 56–60.

(36) Peterhead Snooker Co Ltd v Strachan 2001 GWD 20–777 (Sh Ct)

After a lease came to an end the landlords sued under various heads, such as dilapidations. One head was for the expenses incurred by them in abortive negotiations for a new lease. **Held**: that this head fell to be disallowed.

(37) Renfrewshire Council v McGinlay 2001 SLT (Sh Ct) 79

In 1978 the Council granted a 21-year lease of a shop at 55 Dundonald Road, Gallowhill, Paisley, to Duncan and Anthony Henderson. In 1990 the tenants assigned the lease to Joseph McMenemy, with the consent of the landlords. In 1993 the defender, McGinlay, took possession. (How this happened is unclear.) The Council discovered this fact the following year. Negotiations ensued for a lease to be granted to McGinlay but these eventually came to nothing. It seems that during this time no rent was paid. In 1997 the Council served a notice to quit, and in 1998 McGinlay removed. The landlords sued for recompense in lieu of rent. The action was dismissed. The chief reason was that it appeared, from the pleadings at least, that McMenemy was still the lawful tenant, and so *prima facie* liable for the rent, and that it is a principle of the law of recompense that it is a remedy available only in the absence of another remedy. The facts of the case are rather puzzling. It is not clear on what basis McGinlay obtained possession, it is not clear why McMenemy was not pursued for the rent, it is not clear what would have happened if he had been, and it is not clear if a direct recompense claim against McGinlay would have been admitted had the Council attempted recovery against McMenemy but without success. Presumably McGinlay must have been liable to someone for something.

(38) Learmonth Property Investment Co Ltd v Jopp Management Services Ltd
2001 GWD 8–301 (Sh Ct)

A lease was irritated, and the owners then sued the former tenants for damages. **Held**: following such cases as *Walker's Trs v Manson* (1886) 13 R 1198 and *HMV Field Properties Ltd v Skirt 'n' Slack Centre of London Ltd* 1987 SLT 2, that, unless expressly so agreed between the parties, a landlord who irritates cannot claim damages in respect of consequential or subsequent losses. Also **held** that damages for pre-irritancy losses can still be claimed notwithstanding the irritancy. Both points are settled law.

(39) Britel Fund Trs Ltd v Scottish and Southern Energy plc
2002 SLT 223, 2002 SCLR 54

A 'keep open' case, turning on the precise terms of the order to which the landlords were entitled. See **Commentary** p 67.

(40) Howgate Shopping Centre Ltd v Pinwise Ltd
2001 GWD 28–1142 (OH)

The pursuers were the landlords of Falkirk's Howgate Centre. They sued GLS 164 Ltd, as tenants, for unpaid rent, and other charges, and also sued Pinwise Ltd, as cautioners. The first defenders did not enter appearance.

There was no formal lease. What had happened is that Messrs Cole & Co, on behalf of the landlords, had sent an offer to Messrs Henderson Boyd Jackson offering to let the unit to the latter's clients, Optchannel Ltd. The offer contained the following clause:

> The lease shall be in accordance with the provisions of the lease docqueted and signed as relative hereto and containing only such modifications and/or additions as may be necessary to comply with the provisions of the missives to be concluded between us in pursuance hereof ('the missives'). The obligations of the Tenants shall be supported by the personal guarantee of Pinwise Ltd . . . in terms of the Lease and your acceptance of this offer *inter alia*, will be on its behalf in respect of such guarantee.

It also provided that:

In the event of an engrossed Lease not having been executed by the Date of Entry then as from that date the terms of the Missives incorporating the said draft Lease shall be effective and binding on the parties as if the Lease had been executed.

Messrs Henderson Boyd Jackson sent an acceptance with just one qualification, which was that the lease would be to Optchannel Ltd 'or their nominee'. This qualified acceptance was met by a *de plano* acceptance. GLS 164 Ltd were then put forward as nominees, and their name would have been inserted as tenants in the formal lease, had one ever been executed.

When the landlords sued, Pinwise Ltd put forward a number of defences. One was that the offer had been sent to Messrs Henderson Boyd Jackson as agents for Optchannel Ltd, and the qualified acceptance had also been issued by that firm as agents for Optchannel. Hence, the contract constituted by the missives was purely between Howgate Shopping Centre Ltd and Optchannel Ltd, and Pinwise Ltd therefore could not be liable under it. This argument was rejected. If Messrs Henderson Boyd Jackson were acting for Pinwise Ltd then the latter were bound. If they were not so acting, then Pinwise Ltd were not bound. Whether they were so acting was simply a matter for proof. This was surely the right decision.

Pinwise also argued that, since a qualified acceptance has the legal status of a new offer, they could not be bound by any of the terms of the original offer. In the present case the qualified acceptance comprised only a single clause. This fanciful argument was firmly rejected. The terms of the original offer (except insofar as qualified) are necessarily incorporated into a qualified acceptance.

(41) Scottish Ministers v Trustees of the Drummond Trust
2001 SLT 665, 2001 SCLR 495 (OH)

Is a long lease of forestry land presumptively assignable or unassignable? **Held**: assignable. See **Commentary** p 68.

(42) Legal and General Assurance Society Ltd v Tesco Stores Ltd
2001 GWD 18–707 (OH)

Circumstances in which it was decided that tenants had unreasonably withheld their consent to a proposed development. See **Commentary** p 66.

(43) Clackmannanshire Council v Tullis Plastics Ltd
2001 GWD 16–654 (OH)

The Council were lessees of Cobblecrook Dye Works, East Stirling Street, Alva, Clackmannanshire. The parties were in dispute as to whether or not there was a valid sublease in favour of the defenders, and, if there was, the amount of the rent due. This stage of the litigation dealt primarily with the second issue, on the assumption that a valid lease could be established. The level of the rent due under the sublease was linked to the rent due under the head lease, and the latter itself had rent review provisions. The subtenant had, under the sublease, certain rights to be involved in the rent review process in the head lease. The question was whether an increase in the head rent shortly before the sublease was entered into—an increase in which the subtenant had not been involved— should or should not impact on the level of the subrent. It was held that the pursuer's averments were relevant and should go to proof. The case is a fact-specific one but is illustrative of the sheer complexity which tends to arise when property is leased and subleased.

(44) Perth City Wall Ltd v Smart Events Ltd 2001 GWD 23–871 (OH)

This was a case involving irritancy and violent profits. A lease provided for quarterly rental payments, with an irritancy in the event of 21 days of non-payment. The rent due on 1 May 2000 was not paid. On 10 May the landlords served a notice which purported to irritate the lease if the rent was not paid by 14 May. The defenders did not pay, and the pursuers raised an action for declarator of irritancy, with effect from 25 May, for removing and for violent profits. The action was dismissed as irrelevant. Section 4 of the Law Reform (Miscellaneous Provisions) (Scotland) Act 1985 provides that an irritancy cannot be exercised unless an ultimatum notice has been served. The notice must specify a 'period' by the end of which the rent must be paid, and this period must be the longer of either (i) 14 days from the date of the notice or (ii) the contractual period stated in the lease—here 21 days. Evidently the notice dated 10 May did not comply with this statutory requirement. There is some indication that on 2 June a further notice may have been served purporting to irritate the lease as from 16 June but the details are obscure and the opinion of Temporary Judge T G Coutts QC says little about it. Since the declarator of irritancy failed, the question of violent profits did not arise, but it was held that this claim would in any case have been doomed to fail, since 'a claim for violent profits does not arise while the tenant is contesting (provided he has a *probabilis causa*), the validity of the pursuers' entitlement to terminate the lease'.

(45) Provan v Swan 2001 GWD 22–822 (OH)

A fact-specific case about who was the lawful tenant of Netherinch Farm, Milton of Campsie. (Extending, it was said, to 210 acres—it is striking how hectares continue to be generally ignored in litigation.) John Provan claimed to be the lawful subtenant, holding from the principal tenant, Susan McNarey, and he sought interdict against the various respondents from interfering with his possession. The respondents, for their part, claimed that McNarey's tenancy had come to an end and with it Provan's subtenancy. They claimed that the third respondents, Ace Security Management Ltd, were lawful tenants, holding from the current owners, Netherinch Farm Company Ltd. (The first respondent, Charles Swan, was associated with this company and may himself have been the owner of the property at some stage.) The hearing was about interim interdict. The facts were complex and obscure. One curious feature was that some years previously there had been similar litigation, in which Provan had obtained declarator of his subtenancy and Swan had, it seems, been imprisoned for breach of an interim interdict. Given that Provan had been the lawful subtenant and that there was no evidence to show that his subtenancy had come to an end, and given the other circumstances of the case, the court had no difficulty in granting interim interdict.

(46) Munro v George 2001 GWD 23–843 (OH)

A fact-specific case about whether a tenancy was an agricultural holding or a grazing let. Sarah Munro and Harriet Einsidel were co-owners of the Pityoulish estate, near Nethybridge. They sought interdict and interim interdict against Kirsty and Stephen George from 'conducting agricultural operations' on any part of the estate. Their position was that they had in the past granted grazing lets to Kirsty George. The latter's position was that she had a tenancy under the Agricultural Holdings (Scotland) Act 1991 and therefore had the benefits conferred by that Act. Interim interdict was granted, mainly on the basis that such documentation as was available supported the position of the petitioners.

(47) Unilodge Services Ltd v University of Dundee
2001 SCLR 1008 (OH)

In 1987 Dundee University took a 19-year lease of certain property for use as student accommodation. There was a rent review mechanism, which made reference to 'average percentage increase in rental levied in the year of review by the other universities in Scotland for student . . . accommodation'. At that time there were eight Scottish universities, namely Aberdeen, Dundee, Edinburgh, Glasgow, Heriot Watt, St Andrews, Stirling and Strathclyde. But during the 1990s five more universities were created: Abertay, Glasgow Caledonian, Napier, Paisley and Robert Gordon. The question at issue in this case was whether the rent review clause should be construed as referring to the other universities in Scotland as at the time of the lease or to the other universities in Scotland as at the time of the rent review. Evidently there was no 'right' answer here: a decision either way could be justified. The Lord Ordinary (Macfadyen) preferred the second interpretation.

(48) Flockhart v G A Properties Ltd 2001 GWD 37–1410 (OH)

An office in a tenement was let out to the defenders. The lease provided that:

The tenant shall keep the premises in a clean and tidy condition and clear of all rubbish and in good and substantial repair and condition and as often as may be necessary shall re-build, reinstate or replace the premises or any part thereof to the landlords' satisfaction so that the tenants' liability shall not be limited by the age or state of the premises but that subject to the provisos that the tenant shall not be bound by virtue hereof to effect repairs or rebuilding rendered necessary by:- (a) any latent or inherent defect in the premises or (b) damage caused by any of the risks insured against as provided for in Clause 5.2.1 provided that the tenant has paid to the landlords any monies rendered irrecoverable as a result of insurance vitiations by the tenant.

The pursuer (the landlord) claimed that when the lease ended in 1995 it turned out that there had been structural deterioration. The defenders took issue with the relevancy of the pursuer's averments. A proof before answer was allowed. The opinion of Temporary Judge T G Coutts QC is short, but a few points may be noted.

First, he emphasised the important point that an obligation on a tenant to repair presumptively means only an obligation to effect ordinary, not extra-ordinary, repairs. See *Napier v Ferrier* (1847) 9 D 1354, and *Turner's Trs v Steel* (1900) 2 F 363.

In the second place, he confessed to being baffled as to how a tenant could be bound to effect reconstruction in a tenement:

> It is not clear to me how a tenant could rebuild, reinstate or replace the whole premises, (utilising against the landlord the weaker alternative), when these premises are part of a tenement. The tenant could have no right to interfere with external walls as against the other owners or occupiers of a tenement property. Accordingly, even if it could not be established that the movement of the wall was due to inherent defect at the time the tenant entered into the property, it by no means follows that he could be liable to replace after some general movement of the external wall.

In the third place, he expressed a certain displeasure that the authorities cited to him were exclusively English despite the existence of relevant Scottish authority.[1]

(49) Mearns v City of Glasgow Council 2001 GWD 28–1140 (Sh Ct)

A waterpipe burst in residential property, causing damage estimated at £17,500. Was the landlord liable? See **Commentary** p 65.

(50) Simberg Ltd v Martin Retail Group Ltd
Dundee Sheriff Court, 30 March 2001 (unreported)

A shop at 32 Reform Street, Dundee was let in 1980 for 20 years. The tenants did not remove at the ish and this was an action of removal. The defenders pled that

---

1 Some other cases this year display excessive reliance on English authority, and neglect of Scottish authority, evidently causing puzzlement or irritation in the judges. In *Miller v Clerical Medical Investment Group Ltd* 2001 GWD 25–973 Lord Eassie confessed that 'I was unclear as to counsel's purpose in referring to the English authorities' (para 25 of the transcript). In *Broadway v Clydesdale Bank plc* 2001 GWD 14–552 Lord Macfadyen warned against 'undue reliance on the categorisation developed in the English authorities' (para 27 of the transcript). Most remarkable of all is *Cheltenham & Gloucester plc v Sun Alliance and London Insurance plc* 2001 SLT 1151 in which the Lord President carried out an extensive survey of the institutional writers and the Roman law sources, not a single one of which had been cited to him. English authority is often of great importance, but research, like charity, should begin at home.

no notice to quit had been timeously given and that the lease had therefore been renewed by tacit relocation. It was accepted that there had been no written notice but the defenders were prepared to concede that notice to quit need not be in writing. The main issue was whether such communications as there had been between the parties could be regarded as amounting to clear intimation by the landlords to the tenants that they would have to leave. It was **held** that there had been no such intimation. It was also held that the actings of the parties did not amount to an agreement to waive the possibility of tacit relocation. The case contains a valuable analysis of the law.

(51) Conway v Glasgow City Council 2001 SLT 1472, 2001 SCLR 546 (IH)

This reverses, of consent, the decision of the Sheriff Principal reported at 1999 SLT (Sh Ct) 102, 1999 SCLR 1058, 1999 Hous LR 67 (*Conveyancing 1999* Case (44)). The question of law was whether a resident at a hostel can be required to leave without warning. The original decision of the Sheriff, that such warning is necessary, has now been re-instated.

(52) Robb v Dundee City Council 2001 Hous LR 42 (Sh Ct)

A 'dampness and the law' case. Here the tenant sought to invoke s 79 of the Environmental Protection Act 1990 to compel the landlord to improve her flat, arguing that dampness meant that the property was a statutory nuisance. The action failed. The property was not a threat to health and any dampness was due to inadequate heating.

(53) Galloway v Glasgow City Council 2001 Hous LR 59 (Sh Ct)

Also a 'dampness and the law' case. Here the tenant pursued an action for damages at common law against the landlord for having failed to keep the property in repair. The action was successful, and indeed it rather appears from the report that this was a horror story. The landlords argued, among other things, that they could not afford to keep the property in repair: this argument was rejected.

(54) Spurway v Morrod 2001 GWD 36–1395 (OH)

In August 1999 missives were concluded whereby Paul Morrod agreed to lease to George Spurway property at 29–35 Constitution Street, Leith, for 25 years at an initial annual rent of £45,000. But settlement never took place because of a dispute between the parties as to how much money was due to be paid. Later Morrod intimated that he was rescinding the missives on the basis of breach of contract by Spurway. Spurway sought damages for breach of contract by Morrod, and Morrod counterclaimed for damages for breach of contract by Spurway. A complicating factor is that Spurway averred that he had in fact already been given the keys to the property, that he had already proceeded to change the locks, and that when Morrod rescinded the missives the result was that he, Spurway, had been involuntarily dispossessed. This was a procedure roll debate, and proof before answer was allowed in respect of both the claim and the counterclaim.

One of the points at issue was whether the missives combined with the (alleged) possession by Spurway meant that the lease had already come into existence. An authority cited in this connection was Hunter's *Landlord and Tenant*. Temporary Judge T G Coutts QC commented: 'I pause only to observe that citation of that last authority would appear to occur but rarely in the courts, since the judicial library edition with which I was provided still had its pages uncut.'

Finally, it is of interest that Morrod counterclaimed for five years of rent plus certain other sums. It is not easy to see the legal basis for this. The issue is not discussed to any significant extent in the judicial opinion. It was held in *Salaried Staff London Loan Co Ltd* v *Swears & Wells Ltd* 1985 SLT 326 that if a tenant wrongfully throws up a lease, the landlord may either (i) accept the repudiation and claim damages for breach of contract, or (ii) choose to regard the lease as effective and demand payment of the rent itself. Assuming that that decision was sound in law, Morrod may (depending on the facts as eventually determined) have been entitled to demand rent, but he was not entitled to demand future rent. If the counterclaim was for damages (and it rather seems that it was) then it is difficult to see any reason why the quantum of loss should correspond to any exact multiple of the annual rent, let alone the high figure of five years of rent.

(55) Sutherland v Barry 2001 GWD 38–1431 (OH)

Sutherland leased to Mr and Mrs Barry the Waterfront Bar, Wick. The latter rescinded the lease, and he sued them for unpaid rent, rates and insurance, and dilapidations. They claimed that they were entitled to delay payment of these sums against their own claim against Sutherland for damages for alleged fraud. **Held**: following *Smart* v *Wilkinson* 1928 SC 383, that their delictual claim against Sutherland could not form the basis for retention against Sutherland's contractual claims against them.

[A related case is digested at (2).]

STANDARD SECURITIES AND FLOATING CHARGES

(56) Royal Bank of Scotland plc v Kinnear 2001 GWD 3–124 (Sh Ct)

The facts are not wholly clear but it seems that the RBS sought a warrant under s 24 of the Conveyancing and Feudal Reform (Scotland) Act 1970, even though they knew that the debtor was in the process of selling the property. The sale was carried out and the RBS were paid off from the proceeds, including all arrears. Decree was thus never granted. The question arose as to expenses. **Held**:

by Sheriff Principal B A Kerr, agreeing with the Sheriff, that expenses fell on the RBS, since their application had been premature in the circumstances, even though the existence of arrears was not in dispute. It seems that the RBS regarded this as an issue of principle: since there were substantial arrears they were entitled to raise an action, and should not be penalised in expenses for doing what they had a right to do. This view was rejected. The Sheriff Principal stated that expenses are essentially a discretionary matter and each case falls to be determined by its own facts and circumstances.

(57) Trotter v Trotter 2001 SLT (Sh Ct) 42

This case raises fundamental issues about the nature of a right in security. See **Commentary** p 90.

(58) Broadway v Clydesdale Bank plc 2001 GWD 14–552 (OH)

A house was co-owned by a married couple and their son. They all granted a standard security over it to secure a loan to the family business. When the business failed and the bank sought to enforce its security the pursuer (wife and mother) pled that she had been induced to sign by misrepresentations. See **Commentary** p 92.

(59) Clydesdale Bank plc v Adamson 2001 GWD 27–1082 (Sh Ct)

Mr and Mrs Adamson were directors of a company. They granted a standard security over their house to secure the company's borrowings. When the lender sought to enforce the security, the wife pled that she had signed as a result of her husband's undue influence, and that the bank knew or ought to have known of this possibility, and were thus barred from enforcing against her. This defence failed, chiefly because Mr and Mrs Adamson had seen a solicitor before signing and the bank were entitled to assume that proper advice had been given.

(60) J Sykes & Sons (Fish Merchants) Ltd v Grieve 2002 SLT (Sh Ct) 15

The pursuers (heritable creditors) served a calling-up notice, and subsequently raised an action seeking declarator of their rights, authority to sell etc. The defenders denied that any sum had ever been advanced to them and counterclaimed for discharge of the standard security. See **Commentary** p 96.

(61) Gardiner v Jacques Vert plc 2001 GWD 38–1433 (OH) rev 2002 GWD 5–167 (IH)

Whether interim suspension of calling-up notices would be allowed. See **Commentary** p 96.

(62) Clydesdale Bank plc v Spencer 2001 GWD 17–667 (OH)

Clydesdale Bank were creditors of Smith & Ritchie (1986) Ltd. They had security in the form of a floating charge. Their loan was also secured by cautionary obligations granted by Gavin Thomas Spencer and by Thomas Spencer. What the connection was between the Spencers and the company is not stated: one might guess that they were directors and shareholders. On 2 April 1996 the bank put the company into receivership, appointing Ian Watters of Arthur Andersen as receiver. On 10 May 1996 the whole assets were sold by the receiver to S & R Gravure Ltd. The price paid was not sufficient to pay off the bank, which accordingly claimed against the Spencers. When they did not pay the bank sued them.

Their defence boiled down to this: that the sale of the business by the receiver had been at undervalue, and that the bank knew this, and were accordingly barred from enforcing the guarantees. The story told by the Spencers was that Arthur Andersen had earlier been appointed to look at possibilities of refinancing, but that they and the bank had privately evolved a plan whereby the company would be put into receivership and its assets transferred to a company in which the bank itself would have a large interest, this company being S & R Gravure Ltd. The details of this alleged plan are complex, and are merely sketched here. It does of course happen sometimes that a firm of accountants is called in to advise on financial difficulties, that soon thereafter the company goes into receivership (or administration) and that the same firm (or to be precise a partner) is appointed receiver (or administrator). This pattern of events sometimes looks suspicious to those involved with the company in question. The case at this stage concerned the relevancy of the pleadings: they were held relevant and a proof was ordered.

The opinion of the Lord Ordinary (Macfadyen) is of importance because of its discussion of the duties of a receiver and of a chargeholder. He confirms what was already generally accepted, that a receiver is subject to the common law duty incumbent on a security holder who realises the security to achieve the best price reasonably obtainable. He confirms that since a receiver is not, as a matter of law, the agent of the chargeholder, it follows that a breach of duty by the receiver cannot, without more, be laid at the door of the chargeholder, so that, for example, if a receiver sells at undervalue the chargeholder has presumptively no responsibility for that fact. Hence the fact, if it is a fact, that a receiver has sold at undervalue is not normally a defence available to a guarantor who is being sued by the chargeholder. However, Lord Macfadyen goes on to observe (para 23 of the transcript) that a

> floating charge holder, in seeking to enforce the guarantee, [is under a duty] to act in good faith. Good faith does not . . . permit the floating charge holder who has involved himself in a scheme for realisation of the assets attached by the charge, where that scheme results in realisation of the assets at less than their true value, to look to the guarantor to make good the deficiency left by that under-realisation.

The rise and rise of the concept of good faith over the past five years or so has been one of the significant themes of modern Scots law.

(63) Albatown Ltd v Credential Group Ltd
2001 GWD 27–1102 (OH)

The facts of this case are stated at (8) and there is discussion in the **Commentary** at p 63 and p 91. The following additional aspects of this case are noted below.

The Lord Ordinary (Macfadyen) held that the security was to be regarded as a Form B security. A Form B standard security is one in which the personal obligation is not contained in the security deed itself. Since a copy of the missives was incorporated in the standard security, it might have been thought that this was a Form A security. But the decision is probably correct, in as much as the missives pre-dated the security and the copy in the security deed was for evidential purposes only. It might be added that the Form A/Form B distinction is not of great importance anyway.

The Lord Ordinary remarked that 'what further procedure may require to be followed in the event that the pursuers obtain declarator in the terms sought is not a question which can be determined in this action'. Presumably his concern was how the declarator could be given effect to in the Land Register—assuming, of course, that the defenders would not be so kind as to grant a discharge. The point is indeed rather tricky. Section 18 of the Conveyancing and Feudal Reform (Scotland) Act 1970 has certain provisions as to what is to happen when the creditor will not offer a discharge. There are two possibilities. The first is where the standard security is for a money debt, and in that case the debtor is to consign the sum due. The second is where the security is for an obligation *ad factum praestandum*, and in that case the debtor is to obtain a declarator that the obligations secured have been performed. In either case the debtor is then to register a certificate. (It is perhaps surprising that, in the second case, it is not the extract decree that is registered.) Thus s 18 presupposes (except for standard securities securing an obligation *ad factum praestandum*) that by the time the debtor is unsuccessfully seeking a discharge there will still be a sum outstanding. But of course in the typical case this is not so: what has happened is that the debt was fully paid off long ago. There is thus a gap in the legislation.

(64) Bass Brewers Ltd v Independent Insurance Co Ltd
2002 SC 67 (IH)

Bass Brewers Ltd advanced money to Dalandhui Hotel (UK) Ltd, secured over the Dalandhui Hotel. The Hotel was insured with the defenders in a single policy naming both the owners and the lenders as the insured. When it was severely damaged by fire, the pursuers (the lenders) sued to recover under the policy. The defenders had a number of defences. One was that the policy was vitiated by the alleged fraud of the owners. This defence was repelled: any fraud by the owners could not affect the rights of the lenders. Another defence was that the policy required timeous notification of possible claims, and the pursuers had not reported timeously. The pursuers replied that the owners had made a timeous report. **Held**: that the defence was valid, and the report by the owners was not sufficient to meet the separate obligation on the pursuers to report.

SURVEYORS

(65) Howes v Crombie 2001 SCLR 921 (OH)

A consulting engineer issued a report and was later sued by a person to whom the property was sold. See **Commentary** p 115.

(66) Harrison v D M Hall 2001 GWD 33–1314 (OH)

The pursuer commissioned a survey of a shop from the defenders. The latter valued it at £25,000 and the pursuer proceeded to purchase it for £20,500. The pursuer then sued for negligence, claiming that the property suffered from damp and rot. **Held**: after proof, that there was insufficient evidence of negligence. There is some discussion of the case at 69 (2001) SLG 203.

(67) Beechwood Development Co (Scotland) Ltd v Stuart Mitchell 2001 SCLR 725 (OH)

The pursuers employed the defender to survey an area of land in Bearsden which was to be developed. On the basis of the survey the pursuers designed the project and obtained planning permission. At this stage it emerged that the survey was inaccurate in that it mislocated a burn called the Manse Burn. The pursuers' plans were thus disrupted. The case was about quantification of loss.

(68) Bank of Scotland v Fuller Peiser 2001 GWD 37–1411 (OH)

A survey report issued to a purchaser was relied on by lenders, who later sued the surveyors for alleged negligence in preparing the survey report. See **Commentary** p 115.

SOLICITORS AND ESTATE AGENTS

(69) Smith v Lindsay & Kirk (No 2) 2002 SLT 335

James and Patricia Smith concluded missives for the purchase of Millden Steading, Balmeadie, Aberdeen, from a Mr Cameron. The missives obliged the seller to carry out extensive works. A clause in the missives provided that they would cease to be enforceable after two years. Mr Cameron did not do the works. The Smiths suffered certain losses. Among other things, because they could not move out of their existing house they were sued for breach of contract by Carroll and Young, to whom they had sold it on missives. They hoped in turn to sue Cameron for breach of contract, but by the time the two-year deadline had passed no action had been raised. They sued Messrs Lindsay & Kirk for damages for having failed to raise the action timeously. The defenders argued that though they were handling the defence to the action against the Smiths by Carroll and Young, they were not acting for the Smiths in the claim against Cameron.

The debate in the case was reported earlier: 1998 SLT 1096, 1998 SCLR 572 (OH), 2000 SLT 287 (IH) (*Conveyancing 1999* Case (6) and pp 41–42). The present report is concerned with the proof. **Held**: that the defenders were indeed acting in the claim against Cameron. The remainder of the case was concerned with quantum, which was finally set at £5000 plus interest at 8% since 1993.

(70) Newcastle Building Society v Paterson Robertson & Graham
2001 SC 734, 2001 SCLR 737 (OH)

According to the pursuers, in 1993 they made a loan of £135,000 to a Mr and Mrs Hives to enable them to buy Flat 1, 11 Cleveden Road, Glasgow, at a price of £150,000, and they instructed the defenders to act for them, as well as for the borrowers. There were, they averred, various conditions attached to the loan, such as the purposes for which it was to be used, and also that the purchasers were not owners of other property. They averred that there was later default and that they sold the property at a loss. They further averred that (in the words of the Lord Ordinary, Reed, at p 736A):

> They then discovered that the borrowers had not in fact purchased the subjects on 2 February 1993. The entire property at 11 Cleveden Road (a large house on a number of floors) had been purchased by them in March 1991 for a price of £179,000. The house had thereafter been converted into flats. In February 1993 there was no purchase or sale of Flat 1. There was no purchase price of £150,000. The loan monies were used for other (unspecified) purposes.

The defenders, they averred, had reported to them that all the conditions of the loan had been complied with. They claimed that the defenders were in breach of their obligations, both in contract and in delict, and sued for losses calculated at £90,545. The defenders argued (again in the words of the Lord Ordinary, at p 737A):

> that the loss for which the pursuers sought compensation in damages had not been suffered by them as a result of the defenders' breach of their contractual or delictual obligations. The loss which the pursuers sought to recover was the consequence of the borrowers' default. There was no averment suggesting that the defenders had misled the pursuers as to the value of the subjects or the creditworthiness of the borrowers. In any event, the defenders had not warranted the creditworthiness of the borrowers; but the pursuers were seeking to hold the defenders liable for the entire debt on the loan account, as if the risk of the borrowers' default had been assumed by the defenders.

The Lord Ordinary did not accept this approach, and allowed a proof before answer (p 739E):

> If . . . the pursuers would not have advanced the loan, and therefore would not have suffered the loss arising from the borrowers' default, unless they had relied upon the defenders' negligent report, and if the defenders' duty of care existed precisely to protect the pursuers from the risk of default (as may be established in evidence), then there is *prima facie* no reason why the loss should not be regarded as flowing from the breach of duty and as being within the scope of that duty.

(71) Britannia Building Society v Clarke 2001 GWD 18–710 (OH)

This is a decision of some importance as to prescription as a defence to actions of negligence against law firms by lending institutions. See **Commentary** p 102.

(72) G & S Properties v Francis 2001 SLT 934, 2001 SCLR 827 (IH)

The defenders wished to sell their property, known as 'The Doghouse', at Drymen. They approached the pursuers, a firm of estate agents, and signed a contract according the estate agents 'sole selling rights'. This was in May 1996. By April 1997 the defenders had become dissatisfied and they terminated the contract. They put the property in the hands of another firm of estate agents. A buyer was found. G & S Properties demanded commission, and when the defenders would not pay they sued. They lost before the Sheriff and appealed to the Sheriff Principal. They lost again. They appealed to the Inner House, and lost again. At one stage there was a dispute as to whether the pursuers had had a part in introducing the eventual buyers, but it was held that they had not. The question therefore was whether they were entitled to commission even though they had not introduced the buyer and even though the sale took place after the termination of the contract.

The expression 'sole selling rights' is defined in the Estate Agents (Provision of Information) Regulations 1991. The Regulations require an estate agent who uses this form of contract to inform the customer that:

> You will be liable to pay remuneration to us, in addition to any other costs or charges agreed, in each of the following circumstances—
>
> if unconditional missives for the sale of the property are concluded in the period during which we have sole selling rights, even if the purchaser was not found by us but by another agent or by any other person, including yourself;
>
> if unconditional missives for the sale of the property are concluded after the expiry of the period during which we have sole selling rights but to a purchaser who was introduced to you during that period or with whom we had negotiations about the property during that period.

It will be seen that this definition is ambiguous. In the last paragraph does the expression 'was introduced to you' mean 'was introduced to you *by us*' or does it mean 'was introduced to you *by anyone*'? It was held that it means the former. Hence, in the circumstances, commission was not due.

(73) Cheltenham & Gloucester plc v Sun Alliance and London Insurance plc 2001 SLT 347 (OH) rev 2001 SLT 1151 (IH)

In 1990 the Cheltenham & Gloucester granted a loan to a Mr and Mrs Gallacher, to be secured over property in Bishopbriggs. They instructed a solicitor, William Graeme St Clair, to take a 'first charge' over the property. He failed to do so, there being a prior security in favour of the Bank of Scotland. When the borrowers defaulted, the Bank of Scotland sold the property, and no free proceeds were available to meet the indebtedness to the Cheltenham & Gloucester. The latter obtained a decree against the Gallachers for £132,527.88, but apparently this proved more or less unenforceable, because of lack of assets. At this point they claimed from St Clair for breach of contract. When he did not pay they sued him, and obtained decree against him in the Sheriff Court in 1995 for the whole of the bad loan. However, St Clair still did not pay, and in 1997 he was sequestrated.

Now, all solicitors insure, and are obliged to insure, against negligence claims. St Clair was insured, under the Master Policy, with Sun Alliance. He had notified them of the claim against him and to begin with they had defended the action on his behalf. But after a while they withdrew, for reasons which are unclear. At common law the fact that St Clair was insured would have been of little comfort to the Cheltenham & Gloucester, for the indemnity payable under the policy would merely have been added to the general fund available for St Clair's creditors. But this common law rule came to be regarded as unfair, and was changed by the Third Parties (Rights against Insurers) Act 1930. This says that where the insured has liability insurance and becomes bankrupt (sequestrated, liquidated etc), the third party has a direct claim against the insurers. To be precise, s 1(1) and s 1(4) say:

> (1) Where under any contract of insurance a person . . . is insured against liabilities to third parties . . . then . . . in the event of the insured becoming bankrupt . . . if, either before or after that event, any such liability . . . is incurred by the insured, his rights against the insurer . . . shall . . . be transferred to and vest in the third party to whom the liability was so incurred.

> (4) Upon a transfer under subsection (1) . . . the insurer shall . . . be under the same liability to the third party as he would have been under to the insured . . .

Hence the Cheltenham & Gloucester now had a direct claim against the Sun Alliance. This was the present action. Sun Alliance had two lines of defence. The first was that they were entitled to avail themselves of any restrictions there might be in the policy: Sun Alliance could only be liable if the claim arose out of an insured risk. The pursuers fully admitted this, and a proof is to take place. Conveyancers will be interested to know what aspect of the policy Sun Alliance wished to rely on. The policy provided:

> The Insurers will indemnify the Insured . . . against liability . . . for damages . . . in respect of claims . . . made against the insured . . . by reason of any negligent act neglect or omission on the part of the . . . insured . . . occurring or committed . . . in good faith . . .

The defenders argued that the insured had not acted in good faith in that he knew of the prior security held by the Bank of Scotland and had acted deliberately in not obtaining its discharge.

The second line of defence was that the decree obtained by the Cheltenham & Gloucester against St Clair should not be considered as *res judicata* against the Sun Alliance, and that accordingly the latter should be free to plead any defence which St Clair might have successfully pled. At first instance this argument failed

(2001 SLT 347; *Conveyancing 2000* case (63) and pp 116–117) but it was upheld on appeal. Lord Rodger observed that 'the insurance textbooks are curiously silent on the point', but his opinion was that 'the existence of the sheriff court decree cannot, in itself, prevent the defenders from reopening the matter in the present action where the pursuers stand in St. Clair's shoes'. As is common with Lord Rodger, there is a spectacular display of erudition, including citations of Ulpian, Erskine, Bankton and Voet.

(74) G W Tait & Sons v Taylor 2001 GWD 33–1320 (OH)

A law firm settled a negligence claim against it and sought to recover on the basis of unjustified enrichment. See **Commentary** p 105.

(75) Smith v Gordon & Smyth 2001 GWD 26–1066 (OH)

In this case a client sued his law agents for £245,000 for having allegedly failed to give him proper tax advice when he was selling certain property. See **Commentary** p 104.

BOUNDARIES AND DESCRIPTIONS

(76) Royal and Sun Alliance Insurance v Wyman-Gordon Ltd
2001 SLT 1305, 2002 SCLR 34 (OH)

In a break-off disposition land was described by means of (i) a verbal description of the boundaries (ii) measurements and (iii) a plan which was declared to be demonstrative only. On one boundary the verbal description was that the land was bounded by certain other land as described in an earlier break-off writ. That earlier writ was clear, so that it was possible to plot the boundary accurately. The disponees needed to acquire land beyond this boundary, to the extent of a strip some 23.5 metres wide, and eventually did so from neighbours. They then sought to argue (a) that the additional strip was included within the land purportedly conveyed by their disposition; (b) that the disposition was *a non domino* in respect of that strip since it was already part of the neighbouring property; (c) that they had been evicted from the strip in the sense that the neighbouring owners had asserted their rights; and (d) that accordingly they had a claim in warrandice. (The action was in fact raised by assignees of the original disponees but nothing turned on this point.) **Held**: Action dismissed.

The argument turned on (a), ie on whether, despite the clear terms of the verbal description, the other elements in the description were sufficient to carry the additional strip. It was accepted for the purposes of debate that the deed plan included the additional strip, but the plan was demonstrative only and so, it was held, could not prevail against the other elements in the description. That left the measurements. They were consistent with the inclusion of the additional strip, but they were also consistent with its exclusion, because it could not be assumed that the additional land lay to one side rather than to the other of the property. In those circumstances, there was nothing to displace the clear terms of the verbal description.

This decision is another example of a tendency to prefer verbal descriptions over descriptions of other kinds. In the course of argument, however, that preference became entangled in the question of whether or not the verbal description could be treated as bounding. Why this question should be relevant here, when positive prescription was not in issue, was not explained.

(77) Balneaves v Craig
9 April 2001, Stonehaven Sheriff Court, case no A282/93 (unreported)

A seven-year litigation over ownership of a narrow strip separating two properties. The strip was claimed by the owners of both properties, and the defender had begun to construct a building on it until persuaded to stop by the protests of the pursuer. Both parties, in the words of the sheriff, were 'capable of remarkable intransigence'. The strip in question (along with two other small pieces of ground) was contained within the title of both properties. Both were Sasine titles. In those circumstances ownership fell to be determined by possession for the period of positive prescription. **Held**, after a proof, that the pursuer had failed to prove that he (and his predecessors) had possessed the strip for the prescriptive period. The pursuer's main argument was that a garage used by him and his predecessors rested in part on the strip, but the garage had since been demolished and its precise location could not be proved. Accordingly, the defender was assoilzied.

Even if possession by the pursuer could have been proved, ultimate victory would have been with the defender. This was because it was held, on the evidence, that the parties had reached an earlier oral agreement to excamb the disputed strip and the other strips such that the disputed strip was to be conveyed to the defender. Absence of formality fell to be determined under the law in force prior to the Requirements of Writing (Scotland) Act 1995. It was held that the agreement could be proved by the writ of the pursuer (by means of letters from his solicitor), and that the absence of properly executed writing could then be set up by actings of the pursuer amounting to homologation (most notably the construction of a fence round his property in a way that acknowledged the new boundaries that had been agreed).

RECTIFICATION AND REDUCTION

(78) Renyana-Stahl Anstalt v MacGregor 2001 SLT 1247 (OH)

Missives provided that the disposition would include both an obligation on the sellers to reacquire the property in certain circumstances and also an obligation on the buyers to offer the property back in certain other circumstances. In the event the disposition contained the first of those but not the second. When the sellers sought rectification of the disposition to include the missing obligation this was opposed by the buyers. **Held**: Rectification granted. The omission of the obligation was an error rather than the result of a change of mind. See **Commentary** p 74 and p 118.

(79) Cruickshank Botanic Gardens Trustees v Jamieson
2001 GWD 19–735 (OH)

By mistake a disposition conveyed too much land. A subsequent disposition of the same property repeated the error. The original disponers successfully sought rectification of both dispositions to the effect of excluding the excess land. See **Commentary** p 120.

(80) Co-operative Wholesale Society Ltd v Ravenseft Properties Ltd
2001 GWD 24–905 (OH)

A sublease was amended by minute of agreement. Subsequently the landlords of the sublease assigned their lease to a third party. When the tenants under the sublease sought rectification of the minute of agreement, the third party pled s 9 of the 1985 Act (which prevents rectification where it would be to the prejudice of a person who has relied on the deed in its unrectified form). Proof before answer allowed. See **Commentary** p 121.

DILIGENCE AND INSOLVENCY

(81) Souter v Kennedy, 20 March 2001 (unreported) (IH)

For the decision of the sheriff principal, see *Conveyancing 1999* pp 27 and 62–64. It is understood that the appeal against the decision of the sheriff principal was allowed by the Inner House of consent.

RESIDENTIAL CARE FOR THE ELDERLY

(82) Robertson v Fife Council 2001 SLT 708 (IH)

This affirms (by a 2–1 majority) the decision of the Lord Ordinary reported at 2000 SLT 1226 (*Conveyancing 2000* case (84) and p 120). A brief commentary was published at 2001 SLT (News) 186.

When someone needs residential care, who pays? The basic principle is that if the person concerned is able to pay, then s/he should do so, but that if necessary the local authority will pay. There is a means-testing procedure. The National Assistance (Assessment of Resources) Regulations 1992 (SI 1992/2977), as amended, provide that the first £18,500 of the patient's capital falls to be disregarded. But any capital over and above that is deemed available to pay for care fees. Regulation 25 provides that if the person has alienated an asset for the purpose of avoiding liability for fees then that person can be assessed as if he or she still had that asset. In the present case the local authority invoked regulation 25. The main question was whether this meant (i) that they could refuse to provide accommodation for her or (ii) that they had to provide accommodation for her and then seek to recover from her what she was due to pay in the light of having notional capital.

If (ii) was the correct interpretation of the convoluted statutory provisions then the practical effect would most likely be that the local authority would end up paying everything. For how can recovery be made against notional capital? Diligence can be used against actual but not notional assets. Sequestration of the patient would have limited value for the same reason. Sometimes the possibility has been suggested of sequestration followed by reduction of the prior disposal as a gratuitous alienation. The problem here is that a gratuitous alienation by someone who was at the time solvent cannot be attacked, a view now confirmed by Lord Bonomy (at pp 720L–721A):

> Sequestration was suggested by counsel for the petitioner as one possibility. However, sequestration would be pointless unless it resulted in the realisation of assets. Counsel suggested that the disposition of the house might be a gratuitous alienation which could be reduced, thus restoring the actual capital to the control of the petitioner. I consider that outcome to be highly unlikely in view of the provision of section 34(4)(a) of the Bankruptcy Scotland Act 1985 prohibiting the reduction of such a disposition if the debtor can establish that at the time of the disposition, or any time thereafter, her assets were greater than her liabilities.

In the event the First Division adopted interpretation (i). This strengthens the hands of local authorities, by giving them what in most cases will be the only really practical way of enforcing the rule that 'notional capital' must be taken into account.

HUMAN RIGHTS

(83) Strathclyde Joint Police Board v The Elderslie Estates Ltd
2002 SLT (Lands Tr) 2

If the Lands Tribunal varies a land obligation—such as a real burden enforceable by the superior—without awarding compensation to the person whose rights are prejudiced, does that amount to a violation of Article 1 of the First Protocol of the ECHR?

That article says:

> Every natural or legal person is entitled to the peaceful enjoyment of his possessions. No one shall be deprived of his possessions except in the public interest and subject to the conditions provided for by law and by the general principles of international law.
>
> The preceding provisions shall not, however, in any way impair the right of a State to enforce such laws as it deems necessary to control the use of property in accordance with the general interest or to secure the payment of taxes or other contributions or penalties.

The Tribunal granted the application and declined to order compensation to be paid to the superior. The reasoning, however, is perhaps not wholly clear. The Article quoted is generally understood as drawing a distinction between 'deprivation' and 'control'. (Planning law is a good example of 'control'.) 'Control' does not normally give rise to any claim for compensation under the ECHR but 'deprivation' does: there are very few cases in which it has been held that there has been deprivation but that compensation is not due.

Now, one might suppose that if the Tribunal considered that compensation was not due, as it did, the logic would have been that the order being made was merely a question of 'controlling' the use of the superiority. Moreover, there is a strong argument for so saying. The loss of the benefit of a particular real burden is not a loss of the superiority as such. The superiority remains in existence. Yet the Tribunal did not go down that road. It conceded that there had indeed been a 'deprivation'. Nonetheless, it held that no compensation was due. It took the view that Parliament, in enacting the Conveyancing and Feudal Reform (Scotland) Act 1970, had taken into account the respective interests of owners and superiors, and taken the view that discharge of real burdens was justifiable in the general interest.

Right or wrong, the decision will make it harder for those who seek to challenge the Abolition of Feudal Tenure etc (Scotland) Act 2000 under the Article. For the extinction of superiorities will clearly be a 'deprivation'—and yet, on the reasoning in the present case, one that is unlikely to give rise to any claim for compensation.

[Another aspect of this case is digested at (27).]

MISCELLANEOUS

(84) Cahill's JF v Cahill 2001 GWD 31–1252 (IH)

Mr Cahill died in 1986. Problems arose as to the administration of his estate and D J C MacRobert was appointed judicial factor in 1989. The present action, commenced in 1994, was an attempt by the JF to remove the deceased's son from the deceased's house. The defender pled that his occupation was by virtue of an 'arrangement' with the pursuer. **Held**: reversing the Sheriff and Sheriff Principal, that there was sufficient in the pleadings to entitle the defender to a proof of his averments. It was observed by the court that 'the pleadings appear to have been drawn with a view to obfuscating the issues. It is a sad feature of such disputes that even the minds of the lawyers involved tend to become clouded, the issues are never clearly focused and the litigation drags on interminably.' One of the arguments of the defender, a party litigant, was: 'Reference is made to the specific repeated intention of the said Testator when he stated that "James will have the house". It is averred by the Defender that such is in accordance with his late father's cultural Celtic background.'

PART II

STATUTORY DEVELOPMENTS

Note that the full text of all acts and statutory instruments, both Scottish and United Kingdom, is available on www.hmso.gov.uk

TRANSPORT (SCOTLAND) ACT 2001 (asp 2)

This makes provision for joint transport strategies, for bus services (including public/private partnerships), and for road charging. The last of these may have a mild impact on conveyancing. By s 49 local authorities are empowered to make charging schemes for roads in their area. A 'charging scheme' means a scheme for imposing charges in respect of the use or keeping of motor vehicles on roads (s 49(5)). Further details of the content of such schemes are given in s 53. Before a scheme can be made there must be public consultation followed by confirmation by Scottish Ministers (ss 51 and 52). If Scottish Ministers so direct, the local authority may place traffic signs on 'any land' including land in private ownership (s 58).

LEASEHOLD CASUALTIES (SCOTLAND) ACT 2001 (asp 5)

This Act abolishes leasehold casualties, and also abolishes irritancy clauses in most leases granted before 1914. See **Commentary** p 69.

HOUSING (SCOTLAND) ACT 2001 (asp 10)

This received royal assent on 18 July 2001, and some parts commenced on 1 October 2001 (see The Housing (Scotland) Act 2001 (Commencement No 1, Transitional Provisions and Savings) Order 2001 (SSI 2001/336)). When fully in force this Act will make substantial changes to the law, including the right to buy.

As the official Comment on the Act says, 'tenants who currently have the right to buy will continue to do so on existing terms until their tenancy comes to an end. However the rent to mortgage scheme, lender of last resort and fixed price option provisions are repealed, although transitional provisions allow for protection for those currently benefiting from those provisions. The Chapter [ie sections 42 to 52] extends the right to buy to all tenants with a Scottish secure tenancy subject to a number of exemptions in certain specified circumstances. Tenants who did not previously have the right to buy, and all tenants entering into new tenancies, will have the right to buy on the revised terms provided for in this Chapter.' For such tenants the Act 'changes the level of discount to be applied to the market value of the house. It removes the distinction between houses and flats. It sets a new minimum discount of 20% for all those with a five-year eligibility period. It sets a single rate at which the level of discount increases from the minimum, of 1% of the market value for every year beyond five years that the tenant has occupied a house let by a relevant landlord. It reduces the maximum level of discount from 60% of the market value of the house to 35% or £15,000, whichever is the less.' Although the Act extends the categories of tenants with the right to buy, this may not be all that it seems. Quoting the official Comment once more, s 44 has the effect of 'suspending the right to buy for tenants of a registered social landlord. This is intended to ensure that registered social landlords have time to adjust to the new arrangements.'Furthermore s 44(3) 'sets a time period for this suspension of ten years from the date on which the tenancies of the landlord must be Scottish secure tenancies by virtue of an order under section 11(1).'

Other changes include:

- Sections 1 to 10 (partly in force) make certain changes in the law about homeless persons.
- Sections 11 to 41 (not yet in force) restate the rules about secure tenancies.
- Sections 57 to 71 (in force) make detailed provisions about registered social landlords.
- Section 76 (in force) makes new rules about transfers of housing stocks by local authorities and registered social landlords.
- Sections 84 to 87 (not yet in force) provide for the winding up of Scottish Homes and the transfer of its functions, and assets, to the Scottish Ministers.

MORTGAGE RIGHTS (SCOTLAND) ACT 2001 (asp 11)

This received the royal assent on 25 July 2001 and came into force on 3 December 2001. See **Commentary** p 75.

FINANCE ACT 2001 (c 9)

Section 92 of the Finance Act 2001 introduces an important new exemption from stamp duty for land in disadvantaged areas. In Scotland disadvantaged areas are defined by postcode. A list of the relevant postcodes is given in Sched 3 of The Stamp Duty (Disadvantaged Areas) Regulations 2001 (SI 2001/3747), but the list incorporates the Scottish Executive's *Revising the Scottish Area Deprivation Index* (2001; available on www.scotland.gov.uk) and cannot be properly understood without the *Index*. The complete list of postcodes is:

POST CODE	AREA	POSTCODE	AREA
AB1.3	Aberdeen	G40.4	Glasgow
AB2.1	Aberdeen	G41.1	Glasgow
AB2.2	Aberdeen	G42.0	Glasgow
DD1.5	Dundee	G42.7	Glasgow
DD2.3	Dundee	G42.8	Glasgow
DD2.4	Dundee	G42.9	Glasgow
DD3.0	Dundee	G43.1	Glasgow
DD3.7	Dundee	G45.0	Glasgow
DD4.0	Dundee/ Angus	G45.9	Glasgow
DD4.6	Dundee	G46.8	Glasgow/ East Renfrewshire
DD4.8	Dundee	G51.1	Glasgow
DD4.9	Dundee	G51.2	Glasgow
DD11.1	Dundee	G51.3	Glasgow
DG1.2	Dumfries/ Galloway	G51.4	Glasgow
DG9.7	Dumfries/ Galloway	G52.1	Glasgow
EH3.8	Edinburgh	G52.4	Glasgow
EH4.4	Edinburgh	G53.5	Glasgow
EH5.1	Edinburgh	G53.6	Glasgow
EH6.6	Edinburgh	G53.7	Glasgow/ East Renfrewshire
EH8.8	Edinburgh	G66.2	E Dunbartonshire
EH11.3	Edinburgh	G71.5	North Lanarkshire
EH14.2	Edinburgh	G72.0	South Lanarkshire
EH16.4	Edinburgh	G72.7	South Lanarkshire
EH54.5	West Lothian	G73.1	South Lanarkshire
FK2.7	Falkirk	G81.1	W Dunbartonshire
FK8.1	Stirling	G81.2	W Dunbartonshire

POST CODE	AREA	POSTCODE	AREA
FK10.1	Clackmannanshire	G81.4	W Dunbartonshire
G1.5	Glasgow	G81.5	W Dunbartonshire
G3.8	Glasgow	KA1.4	East Ayrshire
G4.0	Glasgow	KA3.1	East Ayrshire
G5.0	Glasgow	KA3.2	E/N Ayrshire
G5.9	Glasgow	KA6.7	East Ayrshire
G11.6	Glasgow	KA7.1	South Ayrshire
G13.2	Glasgow	KA8.0	South Ayrshire
G13.3	Glasgow	KA8.9	South Ayrshire
G13.4	Glasgow	KA18.3	East Ayrshire
G14.0	Glasgow	KA18.4	East Ayrshire
G15.7	Glasgow	KY1.2	Fife
G15.8	Glasgow	KY1.3	Fife
G20.0	Glasgow	KY5.8	Fife
G20.7	Glasgow	KY8.2	Fife
G20.8	Glasgow	KY8.3	Fife
G20.9	Glasgow	ML1.4	North Lanarkshire
G21.1	Glasgow	ML2.0	North Lanarkshire
G21.2	Glasgow	ML2.7	North Lanarkshire
G21.3	Glasgow	ML2.9	North Lanarkshire
G21.4	Glasgow	ML3.0	South Lanarkshire
G22.5	Glasgow	ML4.2	North Lanarkshire
G22.6	Glasgow	ML5.2	North Lanarkshire
G22.7	Glasgow	ML5.4	North Lanarkshire
G23.5	Glasgow	ML5.5	North Lanarkshire
G31.1	Glasgow	ML6.0	North Lanarkshire
G31.2	Glasgow	ML6.6	North Lanarkshire
G31.3	Glasgow	ML6.7	North Lanarkshire
G31.4	Glasgow	PA1.1	Renfrewshire

POST CODE	AREA	POSTCODE	AREA
G31.5	Glasgow	PA1.2	Renfrewshire
G32.6	Glasgow	PA2.0	Renfrewshire
G32.7	Glasgow	PA3.1	Renfrewshire
G32.8	Glasgow	PA3.2	Renfrewshire
G33.1	Glasgow	PA3.4	Renfrewshire
G33.3	Glasgow	PA4.8	Renfrewshire
G33.4	Glasgow	PA14.6	Inverclyde/ Renfrewshire
G33.5	Glasgow	PA15.2	Inverclyde
G34.0	Glasgow	PA15.3	Inverclyde
G34.9	Glasgow	PA15.4	Inverclyde
G40.1	Glasgow	PA16.0	Inverclyde
G40.2	Glasgow	PH1.5	Perth & Kinross
G40.3	Glasgow		

Section 92 needs to be read with The Variation of Stamp Duties Regulations 2001 (SI 2001/3746). The combined effect is to grant exemptions from conveyance on sale stamp duty and from stamp duty paid on a lease premium provided that the consideration (or premium) does not exceed £150,000. A certificate is required (s 92(2)) and this should, as usual, be included in the deed. The Revenue suggests the following:

> I/we hereby certify that this is an instrument on which stamp duty is not chargeable by virtue of the provisions of section 92 of the Finance Act 2001.

In addition it is also necessary to have the usual certificate of value ('does not form part of a larger transaction or of a series of transactions' etc) which (in the Revenue's view) should refer to £250,000 (and not £150,000 as might be thought).

Where the exemption is claimed, the deed still needs to be stamped, though only with a denoting stamp (s 92(3)(a)). Thus, it must be sent to the Stamp Office.

Obviously it is not possible to assess whether the property falls within a disadvantaged area without knowing the postcode. Postcodes can be obtained online (www.royalmail.co.uk/quick_tools/postcodes/).

If a property straddles a disadvantaged and a non-disadvantaged area, the Finance Act (Sched 30, para 1) requires that the consideration be apportioned between the two 'on such basis as is just and reasonable'. Stamp duty is payable in respect of the non-disadvantaged area in the usual way, but no duty will be payable in respect of the disadvantaged area if the apportioned consideration does not exceed £150,000. The Chancellor of the Exchequer announced on 27 November 2001 that the 2002 Finance Bill is likely to raise (or even abolish) the £150,000 limit in respect of non-residential transactions.

The exemption applies to deeds executed on or after 30 November 2001: see The Finance Act 2001, Section 92(8), (Specified Day) Order 2001 (SI 2001/3748). Useful practical guidance can be found in the Inland Revenue's *Customer Newsletter: Disadvantaged Areas Stamp Duty Exemption* (available at www.inlandrevenue.gov.uk/so/disadvantaged.htm).

NATIONAL ASSISTANCE (ASSESSMENT OF RESOURCES) AMENDMENT (NO 1) (SCOTLAND) REGULATIONS 2001 (SSI 2001/6)

NATIONAL ASSISTANCE (ASSESSMENT OF RESOURCES) AMENDMENT (NO 2) (SCOTLAND) REGULATIONS 2001 (SSI 2001/105)

These make a number of amendments to the National Assistance (Assessment of Resources) Regulations 1992 (SI 1992/2977) in relation to Scotland. In particular they increase from £16,000 to £18,500 the amount of capital which can be disregarded in assessing the means of a person requiring residential care. See *Conveyancing 2000* pp 120–123 and *Robertson* v *Fife Council* (case (82) above).

LIMITED LIABILITY PARTNERSHIPS (SCOTLAND) REGULATIONS 2001 (SSI 2001/128)

These regulations authorise limited liability partnerships to grant floating charges.

LAND REGISTRATION (SCOTLAND) ACT 1979 (COMMENCEMENT NO 15) ORDER 2001 (SSI 2001/309)

This extends registration of title to the counties of Inverness and Nairn with effect from 1 April 2002. The only Sasine counties then remaining will be Banff, Caithness, Moray, Orkney & Shetland, Ross & Cromarty and Sutherland, and these are due to become operational areas in 2003.

❧ PART III ❧

OTHER MATERIAL

LAND REFORM (SCOTLAND) BILL

Introduction

This, the flagship legislation of the Executive's land reform programme, was introduced to the Scottish Parliament in the closing weeks of 2001. An earlier discussion draft, with commentary, was published in February 2001 (ISBN 1 84268 914 2). The origins of the bill lie in the extensive consultation exercise embarked on by the pre-devolution Scottish Office in 1997 and culminating in the publication by the Scottish Executive, in July 1999, of a short report on *Land Reform: Proposals for Legislation* (ISBN 0 10 888001 X). The Bill is in three main parts, corresponding to the three quite different topics on which legislation is proposed.

Access rights

Part 1 of the Bill gives to the public at large what is sometimes popularly described as a right to roam but what is referred to in the Bill as 'access rights'. These are rights both to cross land, and also to linger for the purposes of recreation (though not for commerce) (s 1). Access can be taken on foot or by bicycle but not by a mechanically propelled vehicle (other than a motorised wheelchair) (s 9(1)(d), (3)). The new statutory rights are without prejudice to existing access rights, for example rights arising by servitude or public right of way, or the public rights in respect of the foreshore (s 5(3), (4)).

In principle, access rights are exercisable over all land, and also over the foreshore and private (ie non-tidal) rivers and lochs (s 29: definition of 'land'). But naturally there are numerous exceptions, including land under cultivation, ordinary domestic gardens and other land close to a house (the idea being that persons living there have 'sufficient adjacent or associated land ... to have reasonable measures of privacy'), and land developed for sports or other recreation (s 6). In addition, local authorities have powers to restrict or suspend access rights in relation to particular land, although a suspension for 30 days or longer must be confirmed by Scottish Ministers (s 11).

Model rules for the exercise of access rights will be set out in the Scottish Outdoor Access Code. This is to be produced by Scottish Natural Heritage subject to the approval both of Ministers and of Parliament (s 10). A draft was issued for consultation in February 2001 (ISBN 1 84268 960 6). In addition, both landowners and those taking access are directed by the Bill to behave 'responsibly' (ss 2 and 3). Landowners must not attempt to discourage access by notices, fences, animals, or other means (s 14).

Local authorities can provide further regulation in the form of byelaws (s 12). A statutory duty is imposed on local authorities to uphold access rights (s 13), and to draw up a plan for a system of core paths to procure reasonable public access (ss 17–21). A local access forum is to be set up for each local authority area to provide help and advice both to the local authority and to members of the public (s 24).

Community right to buy

Part 2 of the Bill confers on communities a right to buy land as and when it comes on the market. All rural land is potentially available for purchase in this way other than land excepted by statutory instrument (s 30). A 'community' for this purpose comprises all those entitled to vote within the polling district in which the land is situated (s 31(4)). The procedure in outline is as follows. Members of a community can join together to form a 'community body', which is a company limited by guarantee (s 31). The community body then applies to Scottish Ministers for registration of a 'community interest' in respect of particular land (s 34). This is envisaged as happening before the land goes on the market, and must indeed happen prior to conclusion of missives. Ministers have a discretion to accept or reject the application, having taken into account the views of the owners and any heritable creditors, as well as the level of public support (which must normally include a tenth of the members of the community: s 35(1)(d), (2)). A decision must be made within nine weeks of the application. If the decision is favourable, Ministers register the community interest in a new public register known as the Register of Community Interests in Land. Once registration has occurred, the land may not be sold without first notifying Scottish Ministers and giving the community body the opportunity to buy (s 37(1)). Registration lasts five years but can be renewed in the closing six months (s 41).

If the land comes on the market the community body is informed and must indicate its willingness to proceed within 30 days (s 45). It then conducts a poll of the members of the community. A majority of those voting must support the proposed purchase, and usually not fewer than one half must take part in the ballot (s 47). In addition the purchase must be approved by Scottish Ministers. If two community bodies have registered an interest in respect of the same land, Ministers choose between them (s 51). The purchase is initiated by a formal offer made by the community body. The price is the open market value, on certain assumptions, as assessed by valuer appointed for the purpose (ss 52(2), 55(4), (5)).

Crofting community right to buy

A somewhat similar set of procedures is introduced by part 3 of the Bill in respect of croft land. 'Eligible croft land' includes common grazings, salmon fishings and mineral rights but does not include an owner-occupied croft (ie a croft occupied or worked by the landlord or his family) (s 65). Contiguous land which is not croft land may also be bought at the same time in certain circumstances (s 67). The key difference between the part 2 and part 3 procedure is that under part 3 there is no need to wait for the property to come on the market, the right to buy being capable of exercise at any time. This means that there is no need for registration of a preliminary interest—although the progress of applications to buy is logged by a Register of Crofting Community Rights to Buy maintained by the Crofters Commission (s 91).

As with the part 2 scheme, the right to buy is exercised by a company limited by guarantee set up by members of the community. The company is known as a 'crofting community body' (s 68). A 'crofting community' for this purpose means (i) the residents of the crofting township which is situated in or otherwise associated with the croft land in question and (ii) any other tenants of crofts within the township who are resident within 16 kilometres (s 68(3)). 'Crofting township' is defined by reference to shared common grazings (s 68(4)). Further, a resident/tenant is not a member of the community unless he is on the electoral roll for local government elections. Scottish Ministers are empowered to give financial assistance to crofting community bodies (s 87).

The procedure largely follows that in part 2. It is initiated by an application to Scottish Ministers by the crofting community body (s 70). Ministers then take the views of interested parties, including the landowner and the Crofters Commission. A ballot is held of the members of the community, and approval is needed by a majority of those voting and also, and separately, by a majority of those voting who are tenants of crofts within the croft land (s 72). If Ministers approve the application, it is for the crofting community body to 'secure the expeditious exercise of its right to buy' (s 83(1)). The price is the open market value, on certain assumptions, and is fixed by a valuer appointed by Ministers (s 85).

LAW OF FORESHORE AND SEABED

A *Discussion Paper on Law of the Foreshore and Seabed* (Scot Law Com DP no 113; available on www.scotlawcom.gov.uk) was published by the Scottish Law Commission in April 2001. Various proposals for reform of the law are put forward for consultation. The most important is a suggestion that the common law rules on public rights over the foreshore and seabed (which are expressly saved by the Land Reform (Scotland) Bill (above)) should be re-stated in statutory form or otherwise integrated with the new statutory regime proposed by that Bill. Other preliminary proposals include a suggestion that the tidality of a river be defined by reference to the markings on the ordnance survey map, and a proposed rule, for the avoidance of doubt, that deliberate reclamation of land should not affect the ownership of the land so reclaimed.

HERITABLE DILIGENCE

In May 2001 the Scottish Law Commission published its final *Report on Diligence* (Scot Law Com no 183; available on www.scotlawcom.gov.uk). Unlike most Commission Reports, no draft bill is attached, so that some of the detail remains uncertain.

The Report recommends that the diligence of adjudication be abolished, and replaced with a new diligence to be known as 'land attachment'. This is, however, really the old adjudication brought up to date and with a new name. A creditor will be able to register a notice of land attachment in the Land Register (or Sasine Register), the effect of which will be to confer on the creditor a judicial heritable security. After six months the creditor may apply to the court to enforce this security by sale. If the property in question is the debtor's residence, various special protections would come into play, and indeed the Commission leave open the possibility that such property should be exempt from sale altogether.

The Report also makes a number of recommendations for reforming the law of inhibition. Some of these reforms would be more for the sake of clarifying points of obscurity in the existing law than for effecting substantive changes. Other reforms would represent definite changes in the law.

COMMENCEMENT/AMENDMENT OF ABOLITION OF FEUDAL TENURE ETC (SCOTLAND) ACT 2000

A detailed analysis of the 2000 Act is given in *Conveyancing 2000* pp 123–143. For the most part the Act is not yet in force. Commencement will occur in two stages. Part 4 of the Act will be brought into force first, to allow superiors to register notices preserving real burdens. Then the 'appointed day' will be fixed, ie the day on which feudal abolition actually takes place and the rest of the Act comes into force.

An indication of the current thinking of the Scottish Executive in relation to commencement is contained in a parliamentary answer by the then Deputy Minister for Justice (Mr Iain Gray) on 12 November 2001 (S1W–19447):

> [W]e will bring forward the commencement order in due course. The Abolition of Feudal Tenure etc (Scotland) Act 2000 is the first part of our programme of property law reform, and we will assess the appropriate date for commencement when the next Bill in the programme—the Title Conditions Bill—has been enacted. The consultation exercise on the draft Title Conditions Bill concluded on 23 July, and the responses to consultation are being analysed with a view to introduction as soon as an opportunity arises in the legislative programme. Due to transitional arrangements that will have to be made, it is unlikely that either piece of legislation will be fully in effect until two or three years have elapsed.

A full account of the Title Conditions Bill is given in *Conveyancing 2000* pp 75–80. It is likely that, in its revised form, the Bill will make some changes to the 2000 Act. One important change on which the Executive consulted during its recent exercise is the possible removal of the 100 metres rule, ie the rule contained in s 18(7)(a) which (in general) prevents a superior from realloting real burdens to a replacement piece of land unless that land contains a permanent building used for human habitation and resort and lying within 100 metres of the feu.

LAW OF THE TENEMENT

In 1998 the Scottish Law Commission recommended that the common law of the tenement be replaced by a new statutory code. See the Commission's *Report on the Law of the Tenement* (Scot Law Com No 162). A draft Tenements (Scotland) Bill was included as part of that *Report*. At the request of the Scottish Executive the Commission has now revised the draft Bill to take account of the Title Conditions (Scotland) Bill. The revised Tenements (Scotland) Bill may be consulted on the Commission's website (www.scotlawcom.gov.uk).

CONVERSION OF LONG LEASES

In April 2001 the Scottish Law Commission published a *Discussion Paper on Conversion of Long Leases*, inviting views on a scheme to convert ultra-long leases into ownership. See **Commentary** p 70.

SHARP v *THOMSON*

The Scottish Law Commission published a *Discussion Paper on Sharp v Thomson* (Scot Law Com DP no 114; available on www.scotlawcom.gov.uk) in July 2001. In *Sharp* v *Thomson* 1997 SC(HL) 66 the House of Lords sought to solve the problem of receivership occurring during the period between delivery of the disposition and its registration by holding that, following delivery, a disponer ceased to have beneficial interest in the property and that accordingly the property was no longer subject to a floating charge. In *Burnett's Tr* v *Grainger* 2000 SLT (Sh Ct) 116 (discussed in *Conveyancing 2000* pp 93–97) this rule was extended from receivership to sequestration and, by implication, to other insolvency processes also.

The Scottish Law Commission makes a number of criticisms of the approach taken by the House of Lords and puts forward for the purposes of discussion an alternative approach. While the details would vary from insolvency process to insolvency process, the basic idea is that an acquirer would have 14 days after delivery of a deed in which to procure its registration. During this period the acquirer would be unaffected by any insolvency process, including a process which occurred before delivery and of which he was unaware. It is suggested that these protections might be extended to other cases in which ownership is transferred by registration, for example to shares and to certain types of intellectual property.

Whether, or the extent to which, a legislative solution is necessary is likely to depend on the result of the appeal in *Burnett's Tr v Grainger*, which was heard by the Second Division on 12 and 13 February 2002.

IRRITANCY IN LEASES

The protection conferred on tenants in respect of irritancy by ss 4–7 of the Law Reform (Miscellaneous Provisions) (Scotland) Act 1985 was reviewed by the Scottish Law Commission in its *Discussion Paper on Irritancy in Leases of Land* (Scot Law Com DP no 117; available on www.scotlawcom.gov.uk), published in October 2001. See **Commentary** p 71.

NUISANCE HEDGES

Following consultation (see *Conveyancing 2000* p 42) it was announced by the Deputy First Minister, Mr Jim Wallace, on 31 January 2001 that the Scottish Executive accepts the need for a remedy of last resort to deal with high hedges such as leyland cypress (*cupressocyparis leylandii*). The idea is that it should be possible for councils, following a complaint, to require that hedges be cut down. No commitment is given as to when legislation might be brought forward.

ABOLITION OF SCOTTISH CONVEYANCING AND EXECUTRY SERVICES BOARD

As part of the 'bonfire of the quangos' it was announced on 21 June 2001 by the then Minister for Finance and Local Government (Mr Angus MacKay) that the Scottish Conveyancing and Executries Board will be abolished once parliamentary time is found for legislation. The idea is that its function be taken over by the Law Society of Scotland. Details are given in a Scottish Executive document, *Public Bodies: Proposals for Change*. At p 37 it is explained in relation to the Scottish Conveyancing and Executry Services Board that:

> The policy of introducing competition with solicitors in relation to conveyancing and executry services has had very limited success. Of 11 practitioners registered with the Board, only 2 are practising independently of solicitors' firms. It is unlikely that income from registration fees payable by practitioners, and their contribution to insurance premiums, will fully fund the cost of the Board in the foreseeable future.

CONVEYANCING SECTION ON LAW SOCIETY WEBSITE

The website of the Law Society of Scotland (www.lawscot.org.uk) now contains a section devoted to conveyancing. This can be found in the members' pages, under 'Conveyancing Essentials'. The news board is regularly updated and includes, for example, the full text of responses by the Society to reform proposals by the Scottish Law Commission and the Scottish Executive.

CML LENDERS' HANDBOOK FOR SCOTLAND

This was originally issued in July 2000. The *Handbook* is discussed in *Conveyancing 2000* pp 83–86. Two new developments should be noted.

First, it has been announced that the *Handbook* will be amended on an annual basis. The first round of amendments is due in January 2002. The *Handbook* as amended will be available on the CML website (www.cml.org.uk).

Second, a replacement para 5.2.4 has already been issued and applies to new instructions received on or after 1 May 2001. This reads:

> We accept searches from private firms in the Register of Sasines, Land Register of Scotland, Register of Inhibitions and Adjudications, Register of Companies and Register of Insolvencies. Check part 2 to see if we accept property enquiry certificates from private firms. Also check part 2 to see if we accept search insurance—if we do, you must take reasonable steps to check that the policy adequately protects us. You must be satisfied that you will be able to certify that the title is good and marketable. Where we accept the use of private firms, you must take reasonable steps to check that they carry adequate indemnity cover.

LETTERS OF OBLIGATION: CLASSIC AND ROMANTIC

A short article in the *Journal of the Law Society* for April 2001 (p 40) by Alistair Sim of Marsh UK Ltd contains a useful reminder of the distinction between classic and non-classic letters of obligation. A letter is non-classic to the extent that it undertakes to deliver items such as planning permission, building warrants or completion certificates. Such obligations are still covered by the master policy but attract a double Self-Insured Amount contribution, and the amount paid by the insurers is taken into account for discount/loading. By contrast a classic letter attracts no excess. But where such a letter is issued without proper care and inquiry the amount paid by the insurers will be taken into account for discount/loading.

FIRST REGISTRATIONS:
IDENTIFYING THE SUBJECTS ON A NEW PLAN

Paragraph 4.16 of the *Registration of Title Practice Book* begins:

> Frequently the title deeds submitted with the application for registration will contain sufficient information to enable the Keeper to confirm the location, position and extent. If not, the applicant must submit an appropriate, reliable plan.

The Keeper has now issued further guidance in relation to this plan:

The plan should be drawn in conformity with the criteria in appendix 1 to chapter 4 of the *Practice Book*. Subject to the relevant copyright restrictions, solicitors may if they wish base the plan on an extract from the current edition of the Ordnance Map, at the appropriate scale referred to in the *Practice Book*.

The solicitor submitting the plan is responsible for ensuring that the extent depicted on the plan accurately reflects the current occupied extent, and also for ensuring that this coincides both with the extent which the prior titles are believed to support and with the extent which has been possessed for the prescriptive period on the strength of those titles. The Keeper will read the answers to the relevant questions on Form 1 in the light of this responsibility.

The plan should bear a docquet certifying that it depicts the subjects to which the application for registration relates. This docquet should be signed by the granter(s) and the grantee(s) of the deed inducing registration. (Solicitors should particularly note this change of practice: the docquet should no longer be signed by the applicant's agents, but must instead be signed personally by both parties to the transaction.)

The Keeper reserves the right to request further supportive evidence in the course of his examination of title, and—if necessary—to exclude indemnity and/or to restrict the extent of the subjects included in the title sheet.

As before, solicitors can anticipate such problems by attaching a new plan to the deed which induces first registration. The plan should conform to the criteria just described, although only the granter(s) need sign. The reference in the deed should link the plan up both with the description in the titles and with prior possession. The Keeper suggests the following:

All and Whole the subjects delineated/coloured . . . on the plan annexed and subscribed by me/us as relative hereto, which is hereby declared to be taxative and which defines the extent of the subjects possessed by me/us and my/our predecessors in title as [*here insert the description from earlier titles noting any exceptions that are necessary*].

APPLICATIONS FOR REMOVAL OF QUALIFIED MATRIMONIAL HOMES NOTES FROM TITLE SHEETS

If the Keeper is not satisfied as to the position, a note may be inserted on a title sheet to the effect that occupancy rights under the Matrimonial Homes (Family Protection) (Scotland) Act 1981 *may* exist. This note will be removed (and replaced by the standard note under rule 5(j) of the Land Registration (Scotland) Rules 1980) if appropriate evidence is produced to the Keeper. From 1 January 2002 applications for this purpose must be made on form 2 (and not, as sometimes at present, on form 5).

COAL MINING REPORTS ONLINE

Coal mining reports can now be ordered online (www.coalminingreports.co.uk). As well as speeding things up, this allows immediate online confirmation as to whether a coal mining report is required.

STAMP TAXES BULLETIN

The Inland Revenue has announced a new publication, *Stamp Taxes Bulletin*, which is available on the Revenue website (www.inlandrevenue.gov.uk). The first issue, which appeared in July 2001, contains a note on apportionment of heritage and moveables and warns of:

> a steady increase in the number of cases where the amount of consideration attributed to items claimed to be chattels is more than a small percentage of the total consideration. This is especially the case where this brings the chargeable amount just below the £250,000 or £500,000 thresholds. Customers should note that in cases where it appears that an excessive amount of the consideration has been artificially attributed to non-chargeable items a full inventory and breakdown of the consideration will be requested by Stamp Taxes. This is to ensure that all the items claimed as chattels are properly within that description and that the allocation of the consideration is bona fide and not in breach of section 5 of the Stamp Act 1891.

The term 'chattels' means corporeal moveables.

CONSUMERS AND HOUSE-BUYING

In June 2001 the Scottish Consumer Council published a short report on *Consumers and the House-buying Process in Scotland* (available at www.scotconsumer.org.uk). This summarises the results of 630 questionnaires. The survey focused on multiple surveys, the time taken by the house-buying process, gazumping, the service provided by buyers' solicitors, and the possible introduction of a seller's survey. Some 70% of those surveyed were satisfied with the house-buying process in Scotland, and 80% claimed to be satisfied or very satisfied with the service provided by their solicitor. An earlier report by the Scottish Consumer Council in this area (*Home Truths: A Report on Research into the Experiences of Recent House Buyers in Scotland*) is noted at p 43 of *Conveyancing 2000*.

BOOKS

WILLIAM W McBRYDE, *The Law of Contract in Scotland* (2nd edn) (W Green, 2001; ISBN 0 414 01242 9)

KENNETH REID and GEORGE GRETTON, *Conveyancing 2000* (Butterworths, 2001; ISBN 0 406 94302 8)

ROBERT RENNIE, *Minerals and the Law in Scotland* (EMIS Professional Publishing, 2001; ISBN 1 85811 255 9)

JEREMY ROWAN-ROBINSON, ERIC YOUNG, MICHAEL PURDUE and ELAINE FARQUHARSON-BLACK, *Scottish Planning Law and Procedure* (W Green, 2001; ISBN 0 414 014308)

ARTICLES

A D ANDERSON, 'The Land Reform (Scotland) Bill and The Scottish Outdoor Code' (2001) 69 *Scottish Law Gazette* 44

ALAN BARR, 'Something for Nothing?—Rent-free Periods and VAT' (2001) 50 *Greens Property Law Bulletin* 2

DAVID A BENNETT, 'Limited Liability Partnerships—The Conveyancing Aspects' (2001) 54 *Greens Property Law Bulletin* 1

STEWART BRYMER, 'Enforcing Commercial Lease Terms Against Successor Landlords' (2000) 49 *Greens Property Law Bulletin* 4 and (2001) 50 *Greens Property Law Bulletin* 3

STEWART BRYMER, 'Upward-Only Rent Reviews' (2001) 54 *Greens Property Law Bulletin* 3

DAVID CABRELLI, 'The Landlocked Proprietor's Right of Access' 2001 SLT (News) 25

DAVID CABRELLI, 'Overcoming Practical Problems: The Law of Encroachment and the Function of Title Insurance' (2001) 6 *Scottish Law & Practice Quarterly* 137

DAVID CABRELLI, 'Can Scots Lawyers Trust Don King? Trusts in the Commercial Context' (2001) 6 *Scottish Law & Practice Quarterly* 103

ANTHONY DEUTSCH, 'NHBC Agreements and Litigation' (2001) 41 *Greens Civil Practice Bulletin* 2

ISOBEL D'INVERNO, 'Stamp Duty Group Reliefs' (2001) 52 *Greens Property Law Bulletin* 6 and 53 *Greens Property Law Bulletin* 6

MICHAEL FLEMING, 'Recovery of Possession of Heritable Property from Unauthorised Users' (2001) 42 *Greens Civil Practice Bulletin* 5

GEORGE L GRETTON, 'Equitable Ownership in Scots Law?' (2001) 5 *Edinburgh Law Review* 73

GEORGE L GRETTON, 'The Integrity of Property Law and of the Property Registers' 2001 SLT (News) 135

SIMON HALLIDAY, 'Tacit Relocation' 2001 *Juridical Review* 201

MARK HIGGINS, '2001—A Base (Rate) Odyssey' 2001 SLT (News) 273

CAROLINE JAMES, 'Land Registry: Time to re-think conveyancing customs' (2001) 46 *Journal of the Law Society of Scotland* Oct/28

GLYNICE KILPATRICK, 'Ejection in the Court of Session' (2001) 40 *Greens Civil Practice Bulletin* 5

DEANNA LEVINE, 'Legal responsibilities for gas safety' (2001) 46 *Journal of the Law Society of Scotland* Feb/35

LINSEY LEWIN and STEWART BRYMER, 'Stamping of Deeds: Practical Update' (2001) 51 *Greens Property Law Bulletin* 3 and (2001) 46 *Journal of the Law Society of Scotland* June/8)

LINSEY LEWIN and STEWART BRYMER, 'Same Day Value Payments or Telegraphic Transfers—as we would call them' (2001) 55 *Greens Property Law Bulletin* 1

A J MCDONALD, 'Rectification and Indemnity in the Land Register' (part 1) (2001) 55 *Greens Property Law Bulletin* 6

DONNA W MCKENZIE SKENE and JEREMY ROWAN-ROBINSON, 'Access to the Scottish Countryside: Proposals for Reform' 2001 *Juridical Review* 95

MARY MACRAE, 'Septic tanks: taking the lid off' (2001) 46 *Journal of the Law Society of Scotland* March/48

AINSLIE J W NAIRN, 'Scottish Feudal Baronies in Reform' (2001) 69 *Scottish Law Gazette* 46

RODERICK R M PAISLEY, 'Property Law Update' (2001) 6 *Scottish Law & Practice Quarterly* 239

DONALD REID, 'Contaminated Land—Some Initial Reactions to the New Regime' (2000) 49 *Greens Property Law Bulletin* 1

ALISTAIR RENNIE, 'Substitute land and charge certificates' 46 (2001) *Journal of the Law Society of Scotland* Feb/34

ALISTAIR RENNIE and others, 'The Age of E-Conveyancing?' 46 (2001) *Journal of the Law Society of Scotland* June/19

ROBERT RENNIE, 'Boundary Disputes' 2001 SLT (News) 115

ROBERT RENNIE, 'Solicitors' Negligence and the Judgment of Solomon' (2001) 6 *Scottish Law & Practice Quarterly* 95

ROBERT RENNIE, 'Leasehold Casualties' 2001 SLT (News) 235

ROBERT RENNIE, 'Statutory Personal Bar—*rei interventus* Replaced' (2001) 6 *Scottish Law & Practice Quarterly* 197

STUART ROWSON, 'Six Factors for Smoother Security Deals' (2001) 54 *Greens Property Law Bulletin* 5

ANDREW STEVEN, 'Reform of the Law of the Tenement' (2001) 52 *Greens Property Law Bulletin* 4 and 53 *Greens Property Law Bulletin* 3

ANDREW STEVEN, 'Reform of Real Burdens' (2001) 5 *Edinburgh Law Review* 235

SCOTT CRICHTON STYLES, 'Floating Charges and Subsequent Securities' (2001) 6 *Scottish Law & Practice Quarterly* 73

KEN SWINTON, 'Is there a need to reverse *Sharp v Thomson*?' (2001) 69 *Scottish Law Gazette* 156

JOHN URQUHART, 'Mortgage Rights (Scotland) Act 2001' (2001) 53 *Greens Property Law Bulletin* 1

SCOTT WORTLEY, 'Of Inoperative Deeds and Operational Areas' 2001 SLT (News) 79

SCOTT WORTLEY and ANDREW J M STEVEN, 'The Modernisation of Real Burdens and Servitudes: Some Observations on the Title Conditions (Scotland) Bill Consultation Paper' (2001) 6 *Scottish Law & Practice Quarterly* 261

❧ PART IV ❧

COMMENTARY

MISSIVES OF SALE

Negotiations as contracts

Sometimes clients have been in negotiation long before they contact their solicitors. Can such negotiations themselves amount to a contract of sale? Or in other words are parties sometimes in contractual relations even before they set foot in a solicitors' office?

The answer will usually not matter. Whatever the status of prior negotiations, solicitors will take instructions and conclude a formal contract in the usual way. If the negotiations had contractual effect, that earlier contract will be superseded by the formal missives. In technical language there will be novation of the earlier contract.

In one case, however, the answer does matter. This is where, in the interval between negotiations and formal contract, there is a change of heart by one of the parties. Usually a person is not bound until formal missives are concluded; but if there were prior negotiations with contractual effect, the person is already bound and cannot elect to abandon the transaction.

This precise issue arose in *Bogie* v *The Forestry Commission*.[1] Mr Bogie was in negotiation with the Forestry Commission about the acquisition of land in Dumfriesshire for use as a landfill waste disposal site. The negotiations were conducted by professional agents—but not lawyers—on both sides. They ran for some months, and included letters, e-mails and conversations. Eventually it was agreed to refer matters to the parties' solicitors so that formal documentation could be prepared. At this point a public meeting was held to discuss the plans for the site. The degree of hostility took the Forestry Commission by surprise, and they decided not to proceed with the sale until the concerns raised at the meeting had been met. Mr Bogie argued that it was too late for such misgivings and that there was already a contract between the parties.

While prior negotiations are common enough, it is uncommon that they should have contractual effect. This is because three obstacles (at least) must be surmounted before there is a binding contract. The first is form. Admittedly this is less of an obstacle than it once was. In times past a contract for the sale of land had to be adopted as holograph or attested. Today under the Requirements of Writing Act it is sufficient if there is writing subscribed by the maker.[2] An

---

1 2001 GWD 38–1432.
2 Requirements of Writing (Scotland) Act 1995, s 1(2)(a)(i).

ordinary letter will do as long as it is signed. Further, a failure to comply even with this undemanding rule can sometimes be overcome (as under the previous law) by *rei interventus*, now enshrined in statutory form.[1]

The second obstacle is contractual intention. The parties must *intend* to enter into contractual relations, although intention in this context is viewed objectively and is judged by what is said and done and not by what is thought.[2] Negotiations may be no more than that. If it is accepted on both sides that solicitors will eventually have to be involved, exchanges which take place during the pre-solicitor phase may lack the necessary contractual intention. This point might have been, but was not, argued in *Bogie*.

The final obstacle is agreement on the essentials. For a contract of sale to exist there must be consensus as to parties, price and property.[3] It was here that the negotiations in *Bogie* fell down. There was agreement as to parties. But there was held to be no agreement about either price or property. More may be said about the last of these. The negotiations disclosed agreement that there was to be sold about 24 hectares, and that this included an area of 10.58 hectares in respect of which the purchaser had applied for planning permission. But the precise boundaries could not be delineated. One possible way of rescuing the contract, as Lord Macfadyen noted, would be to say that there was a sale of 10.58 hectares plus an additional 13 hectares to be nominated by the sellers.[4] There would then be agreement, if not as to the actual boundaries, then as to the manner in which these boundaries were to be delineated. But the negotiations did not warrant the conclusion that the sellers were to fix the boundaries, and in the event there was held to be no agreement as to the property sold.[5]

One other matter may be mentioned. The alleged contract in *Bogie* was not a direct contract to buy but rather an option to acquire in the future. It was held, however, surely correctly, that the essential elements of an ordinary contract of sale (parties, price, property) apply equally to options.[6] Indeed in the case of options there is not one price but two—the price for the grant of the option and the 'true' price, ie the price to be paid for the conveyance of the property.[7]

Supersession of missives

Missives are no longer automatically superseded by delivery of the disposition. The law here was changed by s 2 of the Contract (Scotland) Act 1997. But just as

---

1 1995 Act, s 1(3), (4).

2 W W McBryde, *The Law of Contract in Scotland* (2nd edn, 2001) pp 89–93.

3 G L Gretton and K G C Reid, *Conveyancing* (2nd edn, 1999) pp 59–64.

4 Paragraph 37 of the transcript.

5 Thus Lord Macfadyen (para 38): 'Although there was agreement on the general location of the subjects, their approximate area and indeed the boundaries of a core part of them, there was no agreement on their precise over all boundaries. Nor was there agreement on a machinery for determining their boundaries without reference to future agreement between the parties. I am therefore of opinion that on that account there was no sufficient *consensus in idem* to constitute a binding contract.'

6 Paragraph 34 of the transcript.

7 Paragraph 26 of the transcript (arguments for the sellers).

it was, before the 1997 Act, common to contract *out* of supersession, so, since that Act, it is now common to contract *into* supersession, in order to prevent obligations lingering on for the 5 years or, in some cases, the 20 years of negative prescription.[1] If a supersession clause is used, it is necessary for the parties to agree on its duration. In general the seller will argue for a short period and the buyer for a long one, reflecting the fact that most obligations in missives are on the seller and not on the buyer. In practice, two years is often accepted as a reasonable compromise. But, as *Albatown Ltd* v *Credential Group Ltd*[2] illustrates, two years may not be enough. And where it is not enough it may be the seller who loses out.

Albatown is indeed a cautionary tale. The buyers not being in funds, it was agreed to settle the transaction on the basis of a standard security, to be granted over the subjects of sale and securing the buyers' obligations under the missives (in effect their obligation to pay the price). At first sight this might seem a safe enough procedure. The missives, however, were subject to a two-year clause;[3] and when two years passed without payment being made the buyers argued that the price had ceased to be due. The court agreed. The missives came to an end on the expiry of two years from the date of entry. There was nothing more to be said. The standard security no longer secured a live debt.

Of course, even if the missives are superseded, the disposition remains; and dispositions always make provision about the price. It might be imagined, therefore, that the disposition would disclose the fact that the price was still due and so form the basis of a claim. Not so, however. The relevant part of the narrative clause read:

> IN CONSIDERATION of the price of SIXTY FIVE THOUSAND POUNDS (£65,000) Sterling . . . paid to us by FEDERAL SECURITIES LIMITED . . . of which sum we hereby acknowledge the receipt . . .

As too often, the standard style was followed, right down to the disarming capitalisation and reference to pounds 'sterling'. That the price had not actually been received seems to have occurred to no one.[4] In such cases quite a common way of handling matters has been for the disposition to narrate full payment, but for the unpaid balance to be conceptualised as a loan by seller to buyer. Thus, if the price is £100,000, and £60,000 is actually paid, the idea is that the seller lends £40,000 to the buyer. The buyer thus does indeed pay the full £100,000. (The £40,000 loan payable to the buyer is set off at settlement against

---

1 Those obligations in missives which relate directly to land prescribe after 20 years. Other obligations prescribe after only 5 although, as another case from 2001 illustrates (*Cole* v *Lonie* 2001 SC 610), if the non-performance is latent the period of prescription does not begin to run until it is uncovered.

2 2001 GWD 27–1102.

3 In fact it was a *non*-supersession clause, since the missives pre-dated the 1997 Act. But the general point is the same.

4 This is not an isolated instance of unthinking use of words of style. No fewer than three such cases were noticed in *Conveyancing 2000*, namely *McCafferty* v *McCafferty* 2000 SCLR 256, *Nottay's Tr* v *Nottay* 2001 SLT 769, and *Bank of Scotland* v *Reid* 2000 GWD 22–858 (discussed on pp 103–105).

the £40,000 balance of the price.) Hence, the narrative clause is correct, and the standard security will contain a simple obligation to repay a loan. Had matters been handled this way, the narrative clause would have indeed been correct—and, since the security would have secured an autonomous loan, the supersession of the missives would have been irrelevant.

A possible remedy, in a situation such as this, is to seek rectification of the missives or, more promisingly, of the standard security itself. Thus, it might be argued that the common intention of the parties was that the standard security should secure payment of the price until such time as it was paid, and that the security should be rectified accordingly.[1] The argument, in other words, is that the security failed to achieve the legal result that both parties intended. There was an error, not in expression, but in expectation. In principle, errors in expectation are capable of being rectified.[2]

Secret rooms

In *Adams* v *Young*[3] the pursuer bought 5 Grange Loan, Edinburgh from the defenders. This flat was a former shop which the defenders had converted. Three years after entry it was discovered that the wall at the end of a walk-in cupboard was a mere partition which, on removal, formed the entrance to a narrow room some 20 feet in length and 4 feet wide. The discovery was unwelcome. While the rest of the flat was smartly decorated, the secret room, in the words of the judgment,[4] 'was half full of waste and building materials which were wet and covered in fungus with an appalling smell. There were pipes dripping with condensation, an old sink containing brown stinking water and a safe'. As well as being unpleasant, all this festering seemed to have led to an outbreak of dry rot. The purchaser sought damages for misrepresentation, averring that it had been falsely represented to him that the property had been fully renovated.

Various issues are raised by these facts but only one will be mentioned here. The room was disclosed in the drawings which accompanied the building warrant. Does a solicitor have a duty to examine such drawings? In *Adams* it was argued for the pursuer that 'examination of the plans was not part of a solicitor's function or capacity',[5] although in the event the argument was not dealt with (and indeed we understand that the pursuer's solicitor had in fact examined the drawings). But if it is the 'function or capacity' of a solicitor to examine a title plan (as clearly it is), it is difficult to argue that there is no corresponding duty to examine warrant drawings. Of course such an examination might reveal little or nothing. At least in residential transactions the solicitor

---

1 ie under the Law Reform (Miscellaneous Provisions) (Scotland) Act 1985, s 8. For new cases on this provision see pp 118–122 below.
2 *Bank of Ireland* v *Bass Brewers Ltd* 2000 GWD 20–786, 2000 GWD 28–1077, discussed in *Conveyancing 2000* pp 118–119.
3 2001 GWD 3–127.
4 Paragraph 5 of the transcript.
5 Paragraph 16 of the transcript.

will not have visited the property and will not be alerted to particular issues. A safer alternative might be to make the drawings available to the client.

LEASES

Liability for losses caused by disrepair

In *Mearns v City of Glasgow Council*[1] a residential property had been let in 1982. In 1997 a pipe burst, causing £17,500 of damage. The tenant sued the landlords for this loss. Evidence showed that the pipe had been defectively repaired at some time before 1982, and it was in a condition in which it might have burst at any time. The landlords were held liable for the loss. The very brief report does not make it possible to follow the court's reasoning in detail. Considerable reliance was placed on an English case, *Summers v Salford Corporation*,[2] whose relevance is perhaps open to question. It should be noted that *Mearns* is not a case about the obligation to repair, but a case about liability for the consequences of disrepair. The common law principle is that such liability is not strict, but arises only out of a culpable failure to carry out repairs. Hence to establish liability, it was necessary to show that the landlords knew, or ought to have known, that the pipe was weak.

Though the report is very brief, it seems that the court took the view that the landlords should have inspected the property in 1982 (citing *Lamb v Glasgow District Council*),[3] and that had they done so then the problem would have been detected. It is not clear whether expert evidence was taken about what sorts of things would normally be checked by a surveyor, and unless evidence was led it is not easy to see how the court arrived at its conclusion. One might also add that the sort of survey that involves detailed examination of everything that might cause a hazard, including the whole plumbing system, is a very expensive sort of survey indeed. Is the law really that every time a property is let the landlord is supposed to incur many hundreds of pounds of survey costs?

There is a sense in this case that the court may be moving in the direction of a new doctrine—that where the landlord is responsible for repairs, there is strict liability for the consequences of disrepair. Whether such a doctrine would be an improvement is arguable. In practice the issue will in most cases be one of whose insurance company must pay. If liability is with the landlord, the cost of the additional insurance premiums will in the long run tend to be passed on to tenants as an invisible component of the rent. Yet most tenants will also be paying premiums for their own contents insurance, so that there will be double coverage. In pure economic theory, the premiums on the contents insurance should be lower because of potential subrogation rights, though whether it would happen that way in practice is unclear.

---

1 2001 GWD 28–1140.
2 [1943] AC 283.
3 1978 SLT (Notes) 64.

Refusing consent unreasonably

It is usually landlords who are charged with refusing consent unreasonably, typically in connection with proposed assignations. *Legal and General Assurance Society Ltd v Tesco Stores Ltd*[1] was the reverse: an unreasonable refusal of consent by tenants. Though the facts are unusual, there is much of interest in the case for the commercial conveyancer.

In 1994 Wm Low Supermarkets Ltd took a 125 year lease of a unit at Faraday Retail Park in Coatbridge. In due course proposals emerged for the enlargement of the retail park by the addition and development of neighbouring ground. This would require the expansion of the car park, which lay within the boundary of the original development. The landlords of the development (Legal & General) were keen on this idea, since they felt that overall trading would improve, and the tenants of the various units were of the same opinion, except for Wm Low Supermarkets Ltd. The latter were a wholly-owned subsidiary of Tesco, and for reasons which are unclear the present action was raised against Tesco, not against the tenants.[2]

A clause in the lease provided that changes to the car park would need the tenants' consent, which consent should not be withheld unreasonably. When this was refused, Legal & General raised an action for declarator, the main element of which was:

> For declarator that the Tenants in a Lease between Faraday Properties Limited and Wm Low Supermarkets Limited dated 5 January and registered in the Books of Council and Session on 23 February, both 1994 in terms of Clause 7.4.4 thereof have unreasonably withheld consent to the alteration of the Tenant's Car Park, as defined in the Lease, which forms part of the development proposal shown on the site layout plan with number 9860 (PL) 001 Rev. H, which is produced.

They were successful. The grounds of the decision are of considerable interest. In the first place, it was held that in such a case consent may be refused only for reasons connected with the lease itself: in the words of the Lord Ordinary (Hamilton) 'refusal for a collateral purpose is bad'. It emerged that the main reason that the defenders were being stubborn was that they had plans to develop the neighbouring ground themselves. That was a collateral reason. In the second place, even if that had not been their main motive, their refusal of consent would have been unreasonable because of disproportionality. Lord Hamilton said:[3]

> It [the tenant] was not entitled to leave out of account the interests of others likely to be affected directly by its decision—in particular, the Landlord and the other tenants of the Park. The first question is whether it was unreasonable for a person in the position of the Tenant and having due regard to those different interests to refuse consent. A related, though apparently separate, question is whether the detriment to

---

1 2001 GWD 18–707.
2 It is difficult to see how any decree against Tesco could affect Wm Low Supermarkets Ltd.
3 Paragraph 50 of the transcript.

the Landlord and the other tenants[1] consequential on a refusal was so dispro-
portionate to any disadvantage to the Tenant as such on a grant that it was
unreasonable for the Tenant to refuse consent. In my view both questions fall to be
answered in the affirmative.

Finally mention may be made of an (English) House of Lords decision from
2001, *Ashworth Frazer Ltd* v *Gloucester City Council*.[2] Here it was stressed that
what is and what is not an unreasonable refusal of consent is not subject to
fixed rules, but falls to be determined according to the facts and circumstances
of the individual case. This might seem obvious enough, but it involved the
overruling of a Court of Appeal decision, *Killick* v *Second Covent Garden Property
Co Ltd*.[3]

Keep open clauses

In recent years, 'keep open' clauses have been at the forefront of commercial
conveyancing litigation.[4] But things seem to be settling down, since 2001 brought
only one such case, *Britel Fund Trs Ltd* v *Scottish and Southern Energy plc*.[5] It
concerned a shop in Dundee's Wellgate Centre, of which Britel were the landlords and SSE the tenants. The landlords obtained an interim order compelling
the tenants to continue to trade from the premises as required by the lease. The
tenants complied with the interim order, and the question was then as to the
precise terms of the final order to be pronounced. The parties were in agreement
as to most of the wording, but the tenants wanted to add a proviso in the
following terms, which the landlords objected to:

> And provided that on the occurrence of a lawful subletting of the whole of the Leased
> Premises (to a party other than a wholly owned subsidiary company of the defenders),
> this interlocutor shall cease to apply to the Leased Premises and on the occurrence of
> a lawful partial subletting (to such a party), this interlocutor shall cease to apply to
> that part of the Leased Premises as is sublet.

The Lord Ordinary (Macfadyen) agreed (i) that the final decree should be
modified on these lines, but (ii) considered the proposed wording of the
proviso to be unsatisfactory and continued the case to enable better wording
to be found. The Lord Ordinary was surely right on both points. The tenants
could not be bound to keep trading themselves if there was a lawful subtenant in the premises, though they could be bound to ensure that the sub-tenant
kept trading. But equally it would not be right to say that the decree would
'cease to apply' in such a case. It would continue to apply, in a modified form,
and indeed would apply in an unmodified form as soon as the sub-tenancy came
to an end.

---

1 The inclusion of the other tenants is noteworthy.
2 [2001] *Times Law Reports* 622.
3 [1973] 1 WLR 658.
4 See *Conveyancing 2000* pp 67–69.
5 2002 SLT 223, 2002 SCLR 54.

Assignable or unassignable?

Whether a lease is or is not assignable is normally a question dealt with expressly in the lease itself, in the clause sometimes called the alienation clause. But occasionally this does not happen, and then the common law must be consulted: at common law some leases are presumptively assignable and some are not. The usual formula is that a lease of unfurnished urban subjects is presumptively assignable, as is an agricultural lease of extraordinary duration, while other leases are presumptively unassignable, except of course with the landlord's consent. In this formula the word 'urban' seems to refer to premises rather than location, so that a lease of an unfurnished building in the countryside would qualify; and though case law has not fully defined 'extraordinary' it is generally regarded as meaning more than 21 years.[1] But there is very little authority, for the simple reason that leases usually have express provision. However, *Scottish Ministers* v *Trustees of the Drummond Trust*[2] was a case where the lease itself was silent and the matter had to be determined according to the common law rules.

In 1967 the Earl of Ancaster granted a 99 year lease to the Secretary of State, for forestry purposes. The subjects consisted of 85 acres at Easter Muirhead Plantation, Muthill, Perthshire. The Drummond Trust was the Earl's successor in title, while as a result of the Scotland Act 1998 the Scottish Ministers now stood in the shoes of the Secretary of State. Although the lease was for 99 years, the landlord had certain break options, but these options were personal to the original landlord and thus had been lost. The lease was silent as to the right to assign. Perhaps back in 1967 nobody envisaged the possibility that the tenant might wish to assign. Scottish Ministers wished to assign the lease to a company called Taxus Ltd. The landlords, who wished to buy out the lease, refused to consent. Ministers responded with the present action, seeking declarator that they were entitled to assign without the consent of the landlords.

The real nub of the case was whether a lease of this sort is, at common law, presumptively assignable or presumptively non-assignable. The landlords argued that the rule that a lease over 21 years is presumptively assignable is a rule applying to agricultural leases, and that this was not an agricultural lease. They argued that the starting point is a general presumption against assignability,[3] and that there was insufficient here to rebut that presumption.

This argument did not prevail. Whilst the Lord Ordinary (Carloway) did not expressly say that 'extraordinary duration' has a unitary meaning, that is the tenor of his opinion. It would certainly be unfortunate if there were a gap in the common law: it would be much more straightforward if the common law rule were simply that all leases over 21 years are presumptively assignable, and the present case comes close to that sensible conclusion.[4]

---

1 See G C H Paton & J G S Cameron *Law of Landlord and Tenant in Scotland* (1967) p 151.
2 2001 SLT 665, 2001 SCLR 495.
3 *Duke of Portland* v *Baird & Co* (1865) 4 M 10 *per* Lord Neaves.
4 However, it may be that the common law has other untidinesses anyway. Thus, mineral leases, for instance, seem to be presumptively unassignable even if for more than 21 years.

This issue is commonly put in terms of whether or not there is *delectus personae*, and was so put in this case. The sceptic may wonder how helpful this is. In any lease, at any rate where the lessee is a natural person, true 'choice of person' (which, after all, is what *delectus personae* means) is intrinsically impossible for the simple reason that the tenant may die before the ish, so that the landlord may willy-nilly be obliged to accept someone else as tenant. The longer the lease, the more inevitable this is, but it is a possibility in any lease. The logic of the *delectus personae* doctrine would be that every lease involving *delectus personae* would end on the tenant's death. But that is not the law—except where the lease itself expressly so provides. Moreover, it is worth noting that the way the Lord Ordinary determined the intentions of the parties went beyond the question of *delectus personae* on the part of the landlord. Thus, he said: 'Given that substantial term, I do not consider that the parties envisaged that the tenants would remain thirled to the land for such a lengthy period with no option to terminate or alienate'.[1] This is sensible, but looks to the interests of the *tenant*, and to the consequent presumed intentions of the parties in the light of those interests. This is not 'choice of person'.

Finally, the pursuers argued that for there to be *delectus personae*, the tenant had to be a natural person, citing *Inland Revenue v Graham's Trustees*.[2] The Lord Ordinary rejected this argument, in our view correctly.

Statutory developments

The law relating to ultra-long leases is in a state of rapid change. The first step was the prohibition of new leases lasting over 175 years. This was s 67 of the Abolition of Feudal Tenure etc (Scotland) Act 2000, and was intended to prevent the development of feudalism by the back door. This provision, unlike most of that Act, is already in force.[3] The second step was taken in 2001, when the Leasehold Casualties (Scotland) Act 2001 was both passed and brought into force. Possible future steps are mentioned below.

Ultra-long leases often make provision for the payment of casualties, on the model of feudal casualties (which were themselves phased out by the Feudal Casualties (Scotland) Act 1914).[4] Casualties are distinct from rent (tack duty). Typically they are payable either on assignation of the lease or at some regular interval such as every 19 years. Usually the amount due is based on the actual rent or some other fixed (and small) sum, but casualties may also be based on rental value (ie on the notional commercial rent for the property for a year).

For much of the twentieth century leasehold casualties were forgotten about and not collected. Indeed, many assumed that they had been abolished. In the closing years of the century, however, a small number of landlords began to

---

1 2001 SLT 665 at 668I.
2 1971 SC (HL) 1 *per* Lord Reid at p 21.
3 For an analysis of s 67, see *Conveyancing 2000* pp 139–141.
4 The 1914 Act in fact contained machinery for the extinction of leasehold casualties too, but this part of the Act was never activated.

enforce payment. In cases where the lease had been registered in the Land Register and references to the casualty omitted, this translated into a claim for indemnity against the Keeper.[1] The result of this sudden activity was hostile publicity and a clamour for a change in the law. The Scottish Law Commission was asked to look into the matter and in April 1998 published its *Report on Leasehold Casualties*.[2] The new Act, a member's bill introduced by Mr Adam Ingram MSP with cross-party support, is substantially based on the Law Commission's draft bill. As well as the Law Commission's *Report*, useful background material on the Act can be found in an article by Professor Robert Rennie published at 2001 SLT (News) 235.

The Leasehold Casualties Act came into force on royal assent on 12 April 2001. All casualties are abolished with effect from 10 May 2000, the day on which the Bill was introduced to Parliament.[3] The landlord can claim compensation from the tenant but must do so by written notice not later than 12 April 2002.[4] Compensation is calculated by reference to tables and multipliers.[5] Usually the base figure is the actual casualty, but for rental value casualties the base figure is the (much lower) ground rent. Casualties already due before 10 May 2000 must still be paid, but s 7 makes clear that the current tenant has no liability for a predecessor's arrears.

Irritancies are abolished for all leases granted before 10 August 1914 for 175 years or more and at a rent not exceeding £150.[6] That encompasses most ultra-long leases. The abolition extends to all irritancies, whether legal or conventional, and in respect of all breaches (and not merely failure to pay a casualty).

Further legislation can be expected. In April 2001 the Scottish Law Commission published a *Discussion Paper on Conversion of Long Leases*.[7] This invites views on a scheme to convert ultra-long leases into ownership. A lease is ultra-long for this purpose if it has an unexpired term of 100 years (or alternatively 175 years). The suggested scheme is an adaptation of the scheme for conversion of feus set out in the Abolition of Feudal Tenure etc (Scotland) Act 2000. On a fixed day (the 'appointed day') all ultra-long leases will automatically be converted into ownership. On the same day the landlord's interest, and all intermediate leases, will be extinguished. The tenant (but not the landlord) can prevent conversion by registering a notice of exemption before the appointed day. The landlord is compensated for loss of rent but must make a claim within a limited time frame. Certain conditions of the lease survive conversion and become real burdens. The process is automatic in the case of conditions concerned with the management and maintenance of (common) facilities ('facility burdens'). Otherwise, conditions will generally survive only if the landlord registers a notice before the appointed day. This must nominate

---

1 *Keeper of the Registers of Scotland v M R S Hamilton Ltd* 2000 SC 271.
2 Scot Law Com No 165.
3 Section 1.
4 Section 2.
5 Section 3.
6 Sections 5 and 6.
7 Scot Law Com DP no 112; available on www.scotlawcom.gov.uk.

other land of the landlord's which is capable of acting as a benefited property in the real burden. Special provision is made for the survival of servitudes.

The *Discussion Paper* also invites views as to whether legislative protection is needed in the case of shorter ground leases, defined as residential leases granted for 50 years or more. Detailed arguments for and against protection are set out at paras 4.6 to 4.21 of the paper. If protection is thought necessary it might take the form of a second conversion scheme—in effect a form of right-to-buy—or of security of tenure. The outline of a possible conversion scheme is set out at paras 4.23 to 4.46 of the paper.

Appendix A of the *Discussion Paper* sets out the results of a survey of some 2679 long leases and gives data in respect of incidence, length, unexpired duration, and rent.

As has been mentioned, irritancy clauses in old leases have, for the most part, been made void by the Leasehold Casualties (Scotland) Act 2001. The majority of irritancy clauses, of course, escape that abolition. But in 2001 the Scottish Law Commission reviewed the rules about leasehold irritancies currently contained in ss 4–7 of the Law Reform (Miscellaneous Provisions) (Scotland) Act 1985: see *Discussion Paper on Irritancy in Leases of Land*.[1] A number of preliminary proposals are set out for the purposes of consultation. It is suggested that the notice procedure for irritancies for monetary breach (usually non-payment of rent) be revised in a number of ways. A statutory form of notice would be prescribed, containing information and warnings. The minimum period of notice would be extended from 14 to 28 days. And there would be new rules as to service to ensure that the notice reaches the tenant. It is also suggested that a notice procedure might be introduced in respect of non-monetary breaches. If so, it would be for the landlord to specify the period within which the tenant is to comply with the obligation (being not less than 28 days), but a different period could be proposed by the tenant in a counter-notice.

Attention is given to the use of irritancy in a case where the tenant has become bankrupt or, in the case of a company, gone into receivership, administration or liquidation. One possible approach would be for irritancy to cease to be competent in such cases—although it would continue to be available if the rent were not being paid or other conditions were being breached. An alternative approach would be to give the trustee in sequestration, receiver, liquidator or other insolvency practitioner a fixed period (for example six months) in which to dispose of the lease without risk of irritancy. In return the insolvency practitioner would adopt all the tenant's obligations under the lease, other than any obligation to trade or occupy the subjects. Such a scheme would be triggered by a notice from the landlord which was accepted by the insolvency practitioner.

Other preliminary proposals include the abolition of legal (as opposed to conventional) irritancies, and the abolition or re-drawing of the common law power of (equitable) relief.

---

1 Scot Law Com DP no 117; available on www.scotlawcom.gov.uk.

SERVITUDES

Parking cars

A servitude of way comprises a right to move rather than a right to stop. But is it possible also to acquire as a servitude a right to stop? More specifically, can a right to park a vehicle be acquired as a servitude? Certainly such 'rights' are quite often encountered in deeds of conditions and elsewhere. Sometimes this is a right associated with a servitude of way—there is in other words the grant of a right to use a road for vehicular access coupled with a right to park one or more vehicles. Sometimes again this is associated with common property. A typical example is an open space attached to a block of flats in respect of which the owner of each flat has a dedicated parking space.

To grant a right is one thing, but to make it effective in a question with successors is quite another. A right is effective against singular successors only if it is a real right, and a right of parking is only a real right if it is a servitude or a real burden. Probably a right of parking can be constituted as a real burden, at least as the law currently stands.[1] The position of servitudes is less certain. There is, at least in theory, a more or less fixed list of servitudes, and only the rights on that list can be servitudes. But in some types of case there is doubt as to whether they form part of the list or not. The right of parking falls into this twilight zone. After an exhaustive examination both of the issues and of the authorities, running to some nine pages, the learned authors of *Servitudes and Rights of Way* (Sheriff D J Cusine and Professor R R M Paisley) have this to say in relation to a servitude of parking:[2]

> Our conclusion is that these authorities are not particularly helpful in that in none of them was the issue directly in point, and therefore no adviser can say with confidence that a right to park will ever be recognised. However, in our opinion, there are compelling reasons for its recognition in some instances.

In a new case, *Davidson v Wiseman*,[3] Sheriff Cusine has now taken the opportunity to help the law along a little. The pursuer claimed that a servitude right of way, including a right of parking, had been established by prescription. In the event the evidence of possession was insufficient for a prescriptive servitude to be established, but Sheriff Cusine accepted the principle of parking as a servitude right. Needless to say his remarks are *obiter*, and the test case is still awaited.

One might ask why the law should be so slow to recognise additional (and generally innocuous) servitudes. The explanation is probably absence of notice

---

1 See K G C Reid, *The Law of Property in Scotland* (1996) para 391. This will cease to be possible once the Title Conditions (Scotland) Bill is enacted and in force. See s 2 of that Bill. As is explained below, the effect of the Bill is that rights of parking will in future be constituted as servitudes. The full text of the draft Title Conditions Bill is annexed to the Scottish Law Commission's *Report on Real Burdens* (Scot Law Com no 181, 2000) (available on www.scotlawcom.gov.uk). The Bill is expected to be introduced to the Scottish Parliament during 2002.

2 D J Cusine and R R M Paisley, *Servitudes and Rights of Way* (1998) pp 179–188.

3 2001 GWD 9–317.

for purchasers. Servitudes can be created by prescription, and even when writing is used the deed need not be registered (although in practice registration almost invariably takes place). Thus, servitudes may exist even when there is nothing on the register. In the language of registration of title, servitudes are overriding interests.[1] By restricting the number of possible servitudes some protection is extended to purchasers. Purchasers cannot tell for sure whether there are servitudes; but they can at least be sure that the range of possible servitudes is limited.

The law, however, is probably about to change. As and when the Title Conditions (Scotland) Bill is enacted and in force, all servitudes created in writing will require to be registered, against both the dominant tenement and the servient tenement. In exchange for this additional formality the fixed list is abolished, and any right which conforms to the general characteristics of servitudes may be created as a real right.[2] There can be no doubt that parking would be included. Of course the change will do nothing for *existing* grants of rights of parking, for the legislation is not retrospective. And nor will it affect rights of the kind litigated in *Davidson*, ie rights acquired by prescription. Here the need to protect purchasers remains and so the fixed list stays in place.

Toilet stops for dogs

Two legs include four. A person exercising a servitude pedestrian right of access can take the dog with him. But what if the dog is badly behaved on the toilet front? What indeed if a main purpose of the journey is so that the dog can be badly behaved? In *Soriani* v *Cluckie*[3] the pursuer was too scared to use her garage and yard because of the neighbours' two dogs, which (it was said) wandered the property and defecated. The neighbour held a servitude right of access. Nonetheless the sheriff decided that access did not include uncontrolled wandering or defecation. Servitudes must be exercised *civiliter*, in the manner least burdensome to the servient owner. That standard had not been attained in the present case.

This victory for hygiene must be kept in context. The rule for open countryside may not be the same as the rule for an enclosed urban yard. And as Professor Paisley points out in a commentary on the case,[4] 'the leaving of such deposits may be a necessary incident of a servitude such as the pasturage of cows or sheep on a field'.

Naming names

Finally, a topic which also spills over into the law of real burdens. In a deed intended to create a servitude or real burden it is best to name names—that is,

---

1 Land Registration (Scotland) Act 1979, s 28(1).
2 Title Conditions (Scotland) Bill, ss 71 and 72.
3 2001 GWD 28–1138.
4 R R M Paisley, 'Property Law Update' (2001) 6 *Scottish Law & Practice Quarterly* 239, 242.

the obligation should be described as a 'servitude' or, as the case may be as a 'real burden'. Indeed as and when the Title Conditions (Scotland) Bill is enacted and in force, it will be compulsory to make mention of 'real burden' or of one of (new) subcategories of real burden such as 'community burden' or 'facility burden'.[1] But sometimes no names are used. This may be because of uncertainty on the part of the drafter as to whether the right in question is properly classified as a real burden or a servitude: in case of doubt leave out. Or it may be no more than an oversight. It is then a question of construction whether the deed is intended to bind successors or whether the obligations so created are merely personal in character.[2]

In *Moss Bros Group plc* v *Scottish Mutual Assurance plc*[3] the deed under scrutiny might possibly have been called a 'deed of servitude' but for the fact that the rights being created were mutual in character. The owners of each of two neighbouring premises in Renfield Street, Glasgow were granted rights of egress over the other property for fire escape purposes. So the deed was called a 'minute of agreement' and the word 'servitude' was nowhere to be found. In due course the owners of one of the premises sold on, and the question became whether their successors had the benefit of the right of egress. That in turn depended on whether the minute of agreement created personal rights or real rights.[4] The operative words were:

> NOW in consideration of the reciprocal rights and obligations granted and undertaken herein Fairdale grants to Scottish Mutual a right of egress from the said subjects belonging to Scottish Mutual from the said openings to the public street over the said subjects belonging to Fairdale and Scottish Mutual grants to Fairdale a right of egress from the said subjects belonging to Fairdale from the said openings to the public street over the said subjects belonging to Scottish Mutual.

These words, taken in isolation, are suggestive of personal rights, for not only is there no mention of 'servitude' but the rights are conferred on the named parties only without reference to successors. On the whole, however, the rest of the deed suggested otherwise. The parties were referred to as 'heritable proprietors', each property was given a full conveyancing description, there was a warrandice clause, and the deed was recorded in the Register of Sasines. Taken together this was enough, in Lord Macfadyen's view, to create a servitude.

As the law currently stands, the rules are much the same for real burdens. One of the issues arising in *Renyana-Stahl Anstalt* v *MacGregor*[5] was whether an

---

1 Title Conditions (Scotland) Bill, s 4(2)(a).
2 For the background law, see D J Cusine and R R M Paisley, *Servitudes and Rights of Way* (1998) pp 120–139 (servitudes); K G C Reid, *The Law of Property in Scotland* (1996) para 390 (real burdens). The treatment in Cusine and Paisley was relied on and applied in the case discussed in the next paragraph.
3 2001 SC 779, 2001 SLT 641.
4 In fact for as long as the other premises remained the property of the original owners, the original personal right remained good and could be assigned with the ownership of the first premises.
5 2001 SLT 1247 at 1259E.

obligation in a disposition placed on 'our said disponees' and not declared to be a real burden might nonetheless bind successors. Unlike *Moss Bros Group* there was nothing else in the deed which pointed to successors being bound. Lord Macfadyen rejected the argument that the bare words 'our said disponees' had the effect of importing the destination from the beginning of the dispositive clause ('their respective executors and assignees whomsoever') and so carried the idea of successors.[1] To import the destination would, as counsel for one of the parties pointed out, require further words such as 'our said disponees *and their foresaids'*.[2] In those circumstances the obligation was said not to be real.[3]

MORTGAGE RIGHTS (SCOTLAND) ACT 2001

Introduction

There are those who thought that the establishment of the Scottish Parliament would mean less English influence in our law. Perhaps that will be so: it is too soon to tell. But the Mortgage Rights (Scotland) Act 2001, at least, shows English influence in two ways. One is the title: one suspects that Westminster would never have dared to pass any Act with such a title.[4] The other is substantive. In England the courts have extensive discretion in connection with the enforcement of mortgages, a discretion wholly absent from Scots law. The 2001 Act was introduced to 'bring Scots law into line with' English law. If that logic is pursued, the time will come when all our law has been 'brought into line with' English law. Perhaps that is what the majority of the Scottish people in fact want.[5]

Of course, the fact that it was English law that inspired the 2001 Act should in itself be no objection, even in the eyes of the strongest legal nationalist. Legal systems, especially small legal systems, are wise to borrow, if they can borrow wisely. And certainly the general principle behind the new Act is to be welcomed. How serious the practical problem was, that is to say the problem of mortgage lenders enforcing their rights in an inflexible and insensitive way, is arguable. But even if the problem was not a major one, it was still worth addressing.

---

1 There is in any case a question as to whether the importation of a reference to 'assignees' can be treated as including future owners. See G L Gretton, 'Heirs, Executors and Assignees' (1984) 29 *Journal of the Law Society of Scotland* 103.
2 2001 SLT 1247 at 1254K.
3 Nonetheless, this being a rectification case, Lord Macfadyen decided that the actual names of the disponees should be inserted after 'our said disponees' so as to make clear, 'for the avoidance of doubt', that successors were not bound.
4 Outside Parliamant the title has caused some irritation. 'Perhaps we should just abandon Scots law now' was Sheriff N M P Morrison's reaction: see (2001) 42 *Greens Civil Law Bulletin* 2.
5 In which case we would be in the minority. In any event, strong pressure is developing for the unification of law throughout the EU. It is not clear how much of even English law will survive 15 years from now.

Residential property only

The Mortgage Rights (Scotland) Act 2001[1] came into force on 3 December 2001.[2] The core idea of the Act is that there should be a substantial element of judicial discretion in the enforcement of standard securities over residential property.[3] The word 'residential' must be stressed. The Act does not affect standard securities over non-residential property. To be precise, the Act applies to 'any standard security over an interest in land used to any extent for residential purposes'.[4] Thus, a standard security over a farm on which stands a farmhouse will be subject to the Act. So will 'buy-to-let mortgages', since it is the nature of the property, not the nature of the secured loan, that is the test.[5] And it is worth pointing out that although in the typical case the debtor will be a natural person, on occasion it will be a company. Indeed, if a company which owns large numbers of residential properties grants a standard security, the Act will apply. But that is not to say that such a company is intended as a beneficiary of the Act. The typical beneficiary of the Act is the person who is simultaneously the debtor in the secured loan, the heritable proprietor of the encumbered property, and the occupier, though, as will be seen, certain other persons can qualify as beneficiaries too.

It's up to the beneficiary to apply

There are many defects in the existing system of standard securities. One of these is that a standard security can be enforced, at least in theory, without judicial process. Given that the object of the 2001 Act is to introduce judicial discretion in the enforcement of standard securities, one might have expected to see the 1970 Act amended so that standard securities could only be enforced by judicial process, and with discretion inserted into that process (except in commercial cases). This opportunity for rationalising the law was not taken. What the Act does is to allow the beneficiary to raise an action her/himself—to be specific, a summary application—asking the sheriff[6] to suspend the creditor's enforcement rights.[7] As well as being an opportunity lost, this gives rise to two unfortunate effects. One is duplication of court process, for the creditor will often have his own action in court. The other is that since the full benefit of the Act can be obtained only by the active step of raising an action, presumably many debtors will never do anything. Since in this world the least deserving are often the most clamant, and the least clamant the most deserving, the result may be

---

1 asp 11. The full text may be consulted on www.hmso.gov.uk.
2 The Mortgage Rights (Scotland) Act 2001 (Commencement and Transitional Provision) Order 2001 (SSI 2001/418).
3 2001 Act, s 1(1).
4 Section 1(1).
5 Other examples noted by John Urquhart are 'a pub or hotel with accommodation for the owner, or the site of a residential caravan'. See (2001) 53 Greens Property Law Bulletin 1 at 2.
6 2001 Act, s 2(7).
7 2001 Act, s 1(2).

that the Act does not work as intended. The debtor with only modest arrears may never get round to applying to the court, especially within the tight deadlines imposed by the Act.

Who are the beneficiaries?

The following are the beneficiaries of the Act, that is to say, those entitled to apply to the sheriff:

(a) The debtor (including joint debtor), provided that the property is his/her main residence.

(b) The proprietor (including co-proprietor), provided that the property is her/his main residence. Of course, in almost all cases the debtor in the secured loan and the proprietor of the encumbered property will be one and the same person.

(c) The debtor's (or the proprietor's) non-entitled spouse (within the meaning of the Matrimonial Homes (Family Protection) (Scotland) Act 1981), provided that the property is that spouse's main residence.

(d) The debtor's (or the proprietor's) heterosexual cohabitant,[1] provided that the property is that person's main residence.

(e) The debtor's (or the proprietor's) homosexual cohabitant,[2] provided that the property is that person's main residence. This extends to the debtor's (or the proprietor's) *former* heterosexual or homosexual cohabitant, where the debtor (or the proprietor) no longer lives in the property but the (former) cohabitant still does, and the parties have a child under 16 who also lives there.[3]

It will be noted that tenanted property comes under the Act in one way but not another. The Act applies to standard securities granted by a landlord of tenanted residential property, but the landlord, though debtor and proprietor, is not a beneficiary of the Act, for the property is not, at least in the normal case, the landlord's main residence—and cannot be if the landlord is a company rather than a natural person. But tenants are not beneficiaries either, for they cannot apply to the sheriff. Hence, it is not obvious why the Act includes standard securities over tenanted residential property at all. It is true that if the property is residential, the heritable creditor has to serve a notice on the occupier, as a condition of enforcement, which is not the case for non-residential property. But the notice is of little value to the tenant.

Children under 16 who live in the property are not direct beneficiaries, but they may be indirect beneficiaries if their parents have parted: this follows from

---

1 'A person living together with the debtor or the proprietor as husband or wife' (s 1(2)(c)).
2 'A person living together with the debtor or the proprietor . . . in a relationship which has the characteristics of the relationship of husband or wife except that the persons are of the same sex' (s 1(2)(c)). This definition throws up some interesting philosophical issues. Which is the husband? And how can *the* characteristics—note that expression—of the relationship between husband and wife exist between persons of the same sex? The definition may also not please those gay and lesbian activists who repudiate 'heterosexism' as a means of defining same-sex relationships. Cf Kenneth Norrie 'Marriage is for Heterosexuals' (2000) 12 *Child and Family Law Quarterly* 363.
3 The child need not be the actual child of the parties: s 1(3).

the definitional scheme of category (e). But in fact *everyone* living in the property is potentially an indirect beneficiary, provided that there exists a qualified applicant, because one of the factors to which 'regard' is to be had when an application is made is 'the ability of . . . any . . . person residing at the security subjects to secure reasonable alternative accommodation'.[1]

Whether those falling within (c), (d) and (e)—current and estranged spouses, and current and estranged cohabitants—will obtain much real benefit from the Act is unclear. For one of the factors to which the court is to have to regard is 'the *applicant's* ability to fulfil within a reasonable period the obligations under the standard security'.[2] One suspects that such persons, who, after all, are not liable for the debt and who are not co-owners, may be reluctant to pay the heritable creditor substantial sums.[3]

Time limits for applying

The Act lays down tight time limits within which an application for a suspension order must be made.[4] If there is a calling-up notice, the application has to be made before the notice has expired, which is to say a period of two months. In this connection it should be noted that the 2001 Act modifies the rule whereby a debtor could consent to the shortening of this period.[5] If there is a notice of default, the application must be made within one month from the expiry of the notice, which is to say within two months from the service of the notice. If the creditor is seeking an order under s 24 of the 1970 Act, or under s 5 of the Heritable Securities (Scotland) Act 1894, the application must be made before the order has been granted.

What the court can—and cannot—do

Once an application has been made, the court can 'suspend the exercise' of the creditor's enforcement rights (most obviously the right to take possession and sell) 'to such extent, for such period, and subject to such conditions as the court thinks fit'.[6] If that sounds broad, it is. No doubt there will soon emerge standard practices.[7]

It should be noted that what the court cannot do is alter the terms of the loan agreement itself. All the court can do is suspend the right to enforce the standard

---

1 Section 2(2)(d).
2 Section 2(2)(b).
3 If they were indeed to pay moneys to the creditor then the question would arise as to whether they could recover from the debtor or proprietor. The issue is complex and will not be entered into here.
4 Section 1(4).
5 But it modifies it only for securities over residential property.
6 Section 2(1).
7 And it may be that English authorities will be looked at, though it should be stressed that the English legislation—contained in the Administration of Justice Acts 1970 and 1973—is by no means the same in its detail. For the English law see eg Edward F Cousins, *Cousins on the Law of Mortgages* (2nd edn, 2001) and E L G Tyler (ed) *Fisher & Lightwood's Law of Mortgage* (11th edn, 2002).

security. All other remedies which the creditor may have remain available, regardless of what decision the court reaches. For example, the creditor remains free to petition for sequestration. Since the property can be sold by the trustee in sequestration, this is a route by which the Act can be circumvented. No doubt the Act will boost the number of sequestrations, but to what extent must be a matter for guesswork. In a sequestration, either the trustee or the secured creditor can sell. As to the former, no doubt creditors will be aware that a substantial element of home protection springs up in the form of s 40 of the Bankruptcy (Scotland) Act 1985. As to the latter, the 2001 Act applies, we think, just as much to a sale by a heritable creditor after sequestration as before.

Another illustration of the fact that an order under the 2001 Act affects only the enforcement rights under the standard security is that the creditor would remain wholly free to enforce any other security, such as an assignation in security of a life assurance policy. Or again, the creditor would remain free to obtain decree for payment and proceed to diligence.

The four legs

The Act sets out four factors which the sheriff is to take into account in coming to a decision.[1] These have been dubbed the 'four legs'[2] and we will use that expression here. They are:

(a) the nature of and reasons for the default,

(b) the applicant's ability to fulfil within a reasonable period the obligations under the standard security,

(c) any action taken by the creditor to assist the debtor to fulfil those obligations, and

(d) the ability of the applicant and any other person residing at the security subjects[3] to secure reasonable alternative accommodation.

These are not separate: they are all factors to which the court is to 'have regard', and there is an overriding proviso that the application cannot succeed unless 'it is reasonable in all the circumstances' to grant it. The third leg is intended to take account of the fact that responsible lenders will often have already taken steps to help the debtor, including postponing the enforcement of the security. One might add that were it not a factor then lenders would be discouraged from giving time and other help to defaulting debtors.

One of the legs is 'the applicant's ability to fulfil within a reasonable period the obligations under the standard security'. But this may prove problematic in practice. Suppose Jack and Jill take out a 25-year loan for £75,000. The loan contract contains an acceleration clause, whereby missed payments give the bank

---

1 2001 Act, s 2(2). These are not, however, intended to be exhaustive.
2 By Mark Higgins, '2001—A Base (Rate) Odyssey' 2001 SLT (News) 273.
3 This category is wider than the category of those who may apply for a suspension order. The children of a debtor, who live with him/her, would be an example of persons whose interests must be considered, but who do not have active rights to seek a suspension order.

the right to call for full payment at once. After three years Jack and Jill default, and the bank exercises its acceleration option, serving a calling-up notice for the whole balance. Suppose that the balance then due is £73,000. Jack and Jill make a mortgage rights application to the sheriff court. What can the sheriff do? What prospect is there that that Jack and Jill will be able to pay off £73,000 'within a reasonable period'? In some cases a remortgage may be possible, and in such cases a suspension order for a short period will make sense. Again, in some cases Jack and Jill may be able to make use of a brief suspension order to sell the house and pay off the creditor from the proceeds. But such cases may not be so common. If a remortgage is possible, then it is surprising that it has not already happened, and the same is true of a sale. So while there will doubtless be such cases, they may not be numerous, and sheriffs will have to deploy their common sense as to whether alleged plans for remortgages or sales are realistic or not.

Parallel problems have arisen in England. The Administration of Justice Act 1970, s 36 provided that the court could exercise its discretion only if 'it appears to the court that in the event of its exercising the power [to suspend the mortgagee's rights] the mortgagor is likely to be able within a reasonable period to pay any sums due under the mortgage . . .' In *Halifax Building Society v Clark*[1] relief was refused to the debtor on precisely this ground—that since the whole of a large debt had become due there was no reasonable prospect of payment within a reasonable time. That case led to the passing of s 8 of the Administration of Justice Act 1973, which provided:

> Where . . . the mortgagor is entitled or is to be permitted to pay the principal sum secured by instalments or otherwise to defer payment of it in whole or in part, but provision is made for earlier payment in the event of default . . . or of a demand by the mortgagee or otherwise, then for the purposes of s 36 of the Administration of Justice Act 1970 . . . a court may treat as due under the mortgage . . . only such amounts as the mortgagor would have expected to be required to pay if there had been no such provision for earlier payment.

Even that provision proved to have its limitations, however, for mortgages securing overdrafts remain effectively outwith the scope of the English provisions.[2]

Now, the Scottish provisions are not drafted in the same way. The 'ability to fulfil within a reasonable period the obligations under the standard security' is not a condition of a suspension order, but merely one of the factors to which regard is to be had. So everything depends on the discretion of the courts. But it is evident that the current wording provides ample justification, in the typical case, for a decision to refuse an application.

Thus far it has been assumed that the whole debt has become due and resting owing, no doubt following on the service of a calling-up notice. If, by contrast, the creditor has proceeded by way of a notice of default, it might appear that there would be no problem, for the creditor is merely demanding that the debtor

---

1 [1973] Ch 307.
2 *Habib Bank v Tailor* [1982] 3 All ER 561.

pay up the arrears. No doubt that is so, though it has to be pointed out that the second leg is actually poorly worded for this case too, for the expression 'the obligations under the standard security' seems to mean the whole debt, not merely arrears.

Registration

If the court makes a suspension order,[1] the order must be registered 'as soon as possible' in the Register of Inhibitions and Adjudications.[2] This is to ensure that both the Keeper and potential purchasers from a heritable creditor will know that the power to sell does not in fact exist. The style of notice has been prescribed by the Mortgage Rights (Scotland) Act 2001 (Prescribed Notice) Order 2001.[3]

Rather curiously, neither the Act nor Order says against whose name the notice is to be registered. Our understanding is that the Keeper's policy is to register against the name of both parties to the application, and also against any other name which may appear to be relevant. In the absence of a definite rule, that is evidently the prudent course of action. But what would a court hold? We would suggest—if the matter ever had to be determined—that the registration should be against the heritable creditor as named in the order. The reason is the general principle of the Register of Inhibitions and Adjudications that entries show limitations imposed on the right of the person in question to sell, or otherwise deal with, heritable property. Where there is a suspension order, the person whose rights are limited is the creditor.

Notices by the creditor

A creditor who wishes to enforce a standard security to which the Act applies must serve certain notices. These can be divided into, on the one hand, notices to debtor or proprietor, and, on the other hand, notices to the occupier.

First of all, notices to the debtor or proprietor. In the case of calling-up notices and notices of default, the 2001 Act amends the statutory forms of notice so that the notice contains information about the right to make an application under the 2001 Act.[4] Thus, no *separate* notice is needed, and creditors must simply remember to use the amended form. If the creditor intends to proceed under s 24 of the 1970 Act (as of course is very common, typically in addition to a calling-up notice) or under s 5 of the Heritable Securities (Scotland) Act 1894, then a separate notice has to be served, again giving information about the right to apply to the court under the 2001 Act. Why a separate notice has to be served on a person to whom service of the action has to be made anyway is unclear.

---

1 It is still unclear whether such orders will come to be known as 'suspension orders' or as 'mortgage rights orders'.
2 2001 Act, s 3. Since suspension orders are property-specific, one might have expected that registration would have been in the Land Register or Register of Sasines.
3 SSI 2001/419.
4 The amendments are in paragraphs 2 and 3 of the Schedule.

Second, notices to occupier. These are always separate notices, addressed to the 'occupier'. Their function is to alert potential beneficiaries of the Act (ie potential applicants) other than the debtor or proprietor about what is happening and about their rights under the Act. It should be observed that these notices to the occupier must be served even if the debtor is in sole occupation. Indeed they must, at least on a literal reading of the Act, be served even if the property is unoccupied. That situation can easily arise. For instance, debtors who see no prospect of meeting their mortgage obligations sometimes just abandon their property. There is evidently a logical difficulty here: how can a notice be served on the occupier of unoccupied property? It may be that if property is unoccupied then it is not property 'used to any extent for residential purposes' with the result that the Act does not apply anyway. But that is speculative, for it could equally well be argued that residential property does not lose its nature just because of a mere temporary interruption in occupation. Another attempt to escape the logical circle would be to say, quite simply, that the Act must be construed purposively, and that it could never have been intended that the heritable creditor must do what is literally impossible.

If the property is not residential property, as defined, then there is no need to serve a notice on the occupier. But if it is residential property then such a notice *must* be served. In the case of calling-up notices and notices of default, the 2001 Act says that unless a notice is served on the occupier then the main notice 'shall be of no effect'. In the case of procedure under s 24 of the 1970 Act or s 5 of the 1894 Act, no equivalent sanction is stated, but it is still said that such notices 'shall' be served. As mentioned above, the requirement seems to exist whether or not there is an occupier other than the debtor and even if there is no occupier at all. It also exists even if there is an occupier, other than the debtor or proprietor, but the occupier is not a beneficiary of the Act, ie is not someone entitled to apply for a suspension order.

Three different kinds of notice to occupier are prescribed. One is for use where there is a calling-up notice or notice of default.[1] The other two are for use where there is an application under s 24 of the 1970 Act or under s 5 of the Heritable Securities (Scotland) Act 1894. If a creditor were, for instance, to serve a calling-up notice and then make a s 5 application, two separate notices to occupier would have to be served.

Rather oddly, the latter two types of notice to occupier contain a paragraph beginning with the words: 'If you are a tenant of AB, in certain circumstances CD cannot take possession of the property without a court order'. Since tenants have no right to seek a suspension order, the purpose of this paragraph is not obvious. Perhaps it is simply to ensure that tenants know what is going on. The words 'in certain circumstances' are difficult to explain, for it is thought that a heritable creditor can *never* evict a tenant without a court order. It is also worth noting that, on general principles, a tenancy will in any case be unaffected by a

---

1 This is inserted as a new Form BB in Sched 6 to the 1970 Act.

heritable creditor's rights if either (a) the tenancy predated the security[1] or (b) was consented to by the creditor. Finally, the 'if you are a tenant . . .' formula for some reason does not appear in the first type of notice to occupier, ie where there is a calling-up notice or notice of default.

The Act says nothing about *when* the notice to occupier must be served. Evidently, the issue is an important one, since if the occupier is a beneficiary of the Act and wishes to apply for a suspension order then time is of the essence. Presumably, therefore, the notice must be served at the same time as service on the debtor or proprietor. This view is supported by the prescribed style to be used where there is a calling-up notice. This informs the occupier that 'you have two months . . . to make an application'.

The notice to occupier must be served by recorded delivery post.[2] This may prove an error. What if the occupier refuses to accept delivery? It has been suggested in the press that well-informed debtors may do so as a means of defeating any attempt at enforcement.[3] It is curious that the Act was drafted in this way, because the 1970 Act itself contains parallel but more workable provisions. Under ss 19(6) and 21(2) of that Act, a calling-up notice or a notice of default may be served either personally or by recorded delivery, and in the latter case if delivery is impossible a form of edictal citation is available.[4]

The interpretation of Acts of the Scottish Parliament is regulated in part by the Scotland Act 1998 (Transitory and Transitional Provisions) (Publication and Interpretation etc of Acts of the Scottish Parliament) Order 1999.[5] Schedule 1, paragraph 4 provides that:

> Where an Act of the Scottish Parliament authorises or requires any document to be served by post (whether the expression 'serve' or the expression 'give' or 'send' or any other expression is used) then, unless the contrary intention appears, the service is deemed to be effected by properly addressing, pre-paying and posting a letter containing the document and, unless the contrary is proved, to have been effected at the time at which the letter would be delivered in the ordinary course of post.

This is the same as s 7 of the Interpretation Act 1978, and, before that, the Interpretation Act 1889, s 26. It is an odd provision in a number of different ways, not least the tension between what is 'deemed' and the proviso at the end, a tension which arguably reduces the whole paragraph to incoherence. There is a body of mainly English case law interpreting it, the general thrust

---

1 See in particular the Leases Act 1449.
2 Sections 4(1) and 4(2)—covering calling-up notices, notices of default and s 24 applications— say that it 'shall' be so served, and s 4(5)—dealing with applications under the 1894 Act—says that it 'must' be so served.
3 See *The Herald* 21 December 2001 under the heading 'Blunder in Mortgage Law will Halt Evictions'.
4 The statute book contains many and varied provisions about postal service. For instance s 4 of the Law Reform (Miscellaneous Provisions) (Scotland) Act 1985 says: 'Any notice served under subsection (2) above shall be sent by recorded delivery and shall be sufficiently served if it is sent to the tenant's last business or residential address in the United Kingdom known to the landlord. . .' This, in its own way, also avoids the problem of non-delivery.
5 SI 1999/1379.

of which is that (i) if a notice has to be served within a time limit, the proviso operates, so that although proof of non-delivery falls on the alleged recipient, such proof is indeed competent, but (ii) if there is no time limit then it is incompetent to offer to prove non-delivery.[1] The 2001 Act, as has been noted, says nothing about when notices to the occupier have to be served, but, as has been argued, by implication they must be served at the same time as service on the debtor. Hence, the conclusion would seem to be that proof of posting is not proof of delivery. Our tentative view, therefore, is that refusal to accept delivery may prevent enforcement. But only litigation will settle this matter. It remains to observe that proof of posting will in any event give rise to a *presumption* of delivery.

Implications for conveyancing practice

It may take some time for the full implications for conveyancing practice to be worked out.

In the first place, a purchaser from a heritable creditor will need to search the Register of Inhibitions and Adjudications to check for any possible suspension order. At present the practice when buying from a heritable creditor is to search against the debtor. In principle the creditor should be searched against too, though this does not always happen when the creditor is a major institution. The question of whose name a suspension order is registered against is discussed above. Whilst the Keeper's practice is, at the moment anyway, to register against all parties having an interest, our tentative view is that the key registration is against the name of the heritable creditor. Hence, in future, the need to search against the heritable creditor becomes even more important.

Next, how long back should the search go? In practice if there has been a suspension order it is likely to have been recent. Moreover, such orders are likely to have a fairly short lifespan. But there does seem to exist a theoretical possibility that an order registered more than five years ago might still be in force. The counsel of perfection would be to search all the way back to the time when the security was granted.

But such a search is not in itself sufficient. A search will disclose whether or not an order has been made. But it will not disclose whether the creditor served the right notices, for it must be remembered that, if the property is of a type to which the Act applies, failure to serve the right notices means that the power of sale does not exist. Hence a purchaser must be satisfied either (i) that the property is not property to which the Act applies or (ii) that the requisite notices were served. It is doubtful whether any modification to missives is required, for the fundamental implied obligation of a seller to provide a good and marketable

---

1 *R v London Quarter Sessions Appeals Committee ex parte Rossi* [1956] 1 QB 682; *Hewitt v Leicester Council* [1969] 2 All ER 802; *Maltglade Ltd v St Albans DC* [1972] 3 All ER 129. An unreported Scottish case of some interest in this connection is *MacLean v Murray*, Fort William Sheriff Court, 11 September 1998. We are indebted to Mr John Macadam of Messrs MacArthur Stewart for this reference.

title will extend to the requirements of the Act. A purchaser who has proceeded reasonably and in good faith will normally be protected.[1] Much will depend on the attitude of the Keeper.

REAL BURDENS

Deeds of conditions

'This deed of conditions', said the sheriff in *Graham & Sibbald* v *Brash*,[2] 'is one of the most badly drafted documents that it has ever been my misfortune to have to try to interpret'. A case-hardened conveyancer, no doubt, would be less easily shocked. But deeds of conditions are not always what they should be.

Part of the difficulty is that such deeds are often drafted well ahead of the development to which they relate. There may be no buildings on the ground, only aspirations, ill-explained by the developers. In that case the deed gets off to a bad start. Worse may follow. The aspirations may not survive the planning process, or the topography of the site. For one reason or another the developers may change their mind. If so the deed of conditions must be changed too before the first property is sold and it is too late. Unfortunately by this time the original deed may have been forgotten about and the need for change not recognised.

Another difficulty is sheer length. Deeds of conditions are long and getting longer. By the time the drafter has reached page 23 s/he may not recollect very clearly what was said in the opening pages. The resulting dangers are obvious. There may be inconsistency between clauses if not outright contradiction. The same thing may be said twice or, sometimes, not at all. Terms carefully defined in the opening clauses may have taken on a different meaning by clause 33. And the dangers are greatly increased if, as sometimes happens, the deed is actually a mixture of several previous deeds each drafted in a different way.

This is not to say that deeds of conditions are always bad. Some are excellent and many others perfectly adequate. Nor is hindsight a fair test of drafting. The question is not what the deed looks like now, in the light of a particular and unexpected problem, but what it looked like at the time it was drafted and having regard to the information which was reasonably available at that time. Nevertheless, and making all due allowances, the overall standard of drafting is not as high as might be wished.

Some errors occur more frequently than others. A common error is a failure to produce accurate definitions. The more elaborate the definitions, indeed, the greater the risk. The worst definition is often of the common parts. To define the common parts as those parts of the site which are unbuilt on is unsatisfactory if nothing has yet been built, if the plans have not yet been finalised, and, worst of all, if the plans are later departed from. For the scope of the definition is fixed at the moment the deed of conditions is registered. Not only does this mean that it

---

1 See s 41, as amended, of the Conveyancing (Scotland) Act 1924.
2 Dundee Sheriff Court, 21 March 2001 (unreported).

cannot be altered by later changes in the development but that, sometimes, that initial scope is unclear or undiscoverable five years hence.

Another common error is a failure to match up the maintenance provisions with those provisions, generally much later in the deed, which deal with meetings, decisions, and the appointment of a manager or factor. Is the first clause subject to the second, so that maintenance can only be carried out if the required number of owners agree? Or can any one owner enforce the maintenance obligations against the other owners? A related area of difficulty is the basis of liability. Almost always, the maintenance clause will impose an obligation to carry out, or pay for, work. But the management clause may sometimes impose a separate, and independent, obligation. And its terms may be different. If so, can both obligations be enforced according to their terms? Or does one give way to the other—and if so, which?

Then there is the problem of omission. Developments are more complicated than ever before. All these new-fangled parts require to be accounted for. At one time the omission was usually of the lift. Provision would be made for the passage and stair but not for the lift. The question would then arise as to whether there was liability for the lift at all, and if so whether it extended to owners on the ground floor who did not use it. Today lifts are common and familiar and the pattern of omission has moved on.

In *Graham & Sibbald* v *Brash* the omission was the swimming pool. The litigation concerned a substantial development in Dundee known as Riverside Green. The swimming pool was for the use of the owners, and was common property (part of the 'common amenity areas') in terms of the deed of conditions. Naturally the pool had various running costs, such as electricity, salaries (for the pool attendant) and telephone charges. When one of the owners refused to pay a share of these costs, he was sued by the managers of the development. The relevant clause provided that:

> The proprietors shall be bound to maintain in good order and repair and when necessary renew the common amenity areas except in so far as any parts of the said common amenity areas have been taken over by the appropriate Local Authority, including without prejudice to the foregoing generality, the replacement of trees and shrubs, the cutting of grass and the sweeping, cleaning and lighting of the Development.

In one sense, of course, the pool had not been forgotten about, because it fell within the definition of 'common amenity areas'. Hence the pool, like the lawn, required to be maintained. But the issue was not maintenance but running costs. A pool can be maintained without being used. Indeed its life would (presumably) be longer if it lay empty, without either water or swimmers. No provision, however, was made for running costs, and the sheriff refused to accept that 'maintain' was capable of bearing the necessary meaning. Real burdens are construed strictly and in favour of freedom.[1]

---

1 The sheriff also took account of the *contra proferentem* rule, although it can be argued that this rule has no application in relation to deeds of conditions which are intended as the governing document for a community and are to be enforced by equals within that community.

Sometimes disaster of the sort just described can be warded off by recourse to the rules of common property. For even if the real burden is ineffective, the facility is at least common property and hence subject to a set of default rules in relation to management and maintenance.[1] But there is no rule of common property that provides for running costs.

In considering issues like this it is important to bear in mind that deeds of conditions cannot usually be altered. Certainly once the first unit is sold off alteration is beyond the power of the developer. And it is beyond the power of the owners too unless everyone agrees, which in practice is rarely achievable. Nor is much help to be found from the courts. An application to the Lands Tribunal will not be accepted unless made by everyone—in which case, of course, it is unnecessary in the first place.[2] And judicial rectification is usually prevented by the fact that new owners have acquired in reliance on the unrectified deed.[3]

Sometimes the deed purports to reserve a unilateral power of alteration to the developer. For example the deed in *Graham & Sibbald* reserved

> to the Superiors the right to alter or modify in whole or in part the reservations, real burdens, conditions, provisions, limitations, obligations, stipulations and others herein contained and in the event of the Superiors so doing the proprietors shall have no right or title to object thereto and shall have no claim in respect thereof.

But it seems improbable that a clause of this kind is enforceable. Nothing is more settled than that the terms of a real burden must be set out in full within the four corners of the deed, and that extrinsic matters cannot form a part of the burden. The most recent example of that rule is *Grampian Joint Police Board* v *Pearson*,[4] discussed below. And the rule cannot, it is thought, be avoided merely by use of the language of variation. To say that the real burdens can be 'varied' by the unilateral act of a third party who is not himself subject to them[5] is tantamount to saying that the content of the burdens is neither fixed nor knowable. It is little more than a blank cheque. But in the law of real burdens all cheques must be completed in advance.

The apparent inability to alter a deed of conditions can be troublesome in practice. A mistake may stand in need of correction. Or circumstances may have changed so that the deed, once perfectly adequate, is no longer so. It is as if the development were governed in perpetuity by a set of bye-laws which could never be changed. Help, however, is at hand. Once it is enacted and in force the Title Conditions Bill will allow a simple majority of owners to alter a deed of

---

1 For which see K G C Reid, *The Law of Property in Scotland* (1996) paras 23—25.

2 *Mrs Young and Others* 1978 SLT (Lands Tr) 28. Of course an individual owner could apply for the variation or discharge of a condition insofar as it affected his or her own property; but the deed would remain unaltered for all other properties, and for that reason the application might well be refused.

3 Law Reform (Miscellaneous Provisions) (Scotland) Act 1985, s 9, discussed at pp 118–122 below.

4 2001 SC 772, 2001 SLT 734.

5 Compare s 31 of the Title Conditions (Scotland) Bill which allows variation by a majority (or other stipulated percentage) of *owners* and the exercise of which is subject to judicial challenge (under s 32). And compare also the clause considered in *Hanover Housing Association Ltd Ptr* 2002 SCLR 144 which likewise requires a majority of owners.

conditions, subject to a right of judicial challenge on the part of any member of the dissenting minority.[1] And the Lands Tribunal is given jurisdiction to vary the deed on the application of a quarter of the owners.[2]

Four corners of the deed

The full terms of a real burden must be set out within the four corners of the deed.[3] *Grampian Joint Police Board* v *Pearson*[4] is the latest case to apply this well-established principle. The dispute concerned a feu charter granted in 1901 for the erection of a police house. It was provided that, if the house was sold for private use, the superiors were to be entitled to buy it back at a price no greater than 'the original cost of said buildings'. At first instance the price was held too vague for the clause to be enforceable.[5] This approach has now been approved on appeal by the First Division.[6]

The First Division accepted that extrinsic evidence might be allowed in some cases in order to shed light on the terms of a burden. But such evidence could not of itself create the burden. 'What is not permissible is to use evidence for the purpose of defining a subject which has not been exactly described.'[7] In the present case, it was said, there was no proper description. '[P]rovision might have been made for a record of the cost to be kept and acknowledged in some way or else the deed could have provided specific machinery for ascertaining the cost'.[8] In the absence of such provision 'the pursuers are being required to look beyond the four corners of the deed to ascertain the extent of the restriction. And that . . . is just what the law will not permit'.[9]

In fact the decision is as much about accessibility as about the principle of expression within the four corners of the deed. Even if the provision had been formulated in the manner suggested by the court it would still have been just as necessary to have recourse to extrinsic evidence. But the evidence would have been readily available. What the court was anxious to avoid was forcing future owners of the house 'to seek for the cost of the police station and, hence, for the extent of the condition affecting their land, among such of the ledgers, account books and other records of the old county council as happen to be extant in Register House or elsewhere'.[10] This suggests a distinction between extrinsic

---

1 Title Conditions (Scotland) Bill, ss 31 and 32. The full text of draft Bill is given in an appendix to the Scottish Law Commission's *Report on Real Burdens* (Scot Law Com No 181, 2000) (available on www.scotlawcom.gov.uk).
2 Title Conditions (Scotland) Bill, s 86.
3 K G C Reid, *The Law of Property in Scotland* (1996) para 388. The rule is reproduced in s 4(2)(a) of the Title Conditions (Scotland) Bill.
4 2001 SC 772, 2001 SLT 734.
5 2001 SLT 90, discussed in *Conveyancing 2000* pp 74–75.
6 It is possible to argue that the pursuers were not truly singular successors. In that case the burden would be valid even if not real.
7 2001 SC 772 at 777B.
8 2001 SC 772 at 778B.
9 2001 SC 772 at 777H.
10 2001 SC 772 at 776C.

evidence which is accessible and extrinsic evidence which is not. A need to use the latter will always invalidate the burden. A need to use the former may or, depending on the circumstances, may not have that effect. So, for example, an obligation to pay a share of the cost of maintenance of common parts is an obligation to pay a sum of money which can only be ascertained by the admission, from time to time, of extrinsic evidence. But the evidence in question (the cost of a particular act of maintenance) is so readily available that the burden is probably not invalid.[1]

The question of when extrinsic evidence may or may not be admissible will always be a narrow one. The same might be said of the question of whether an obligation is sufficiently clearly expressed to be enforceable as a real burden.[2] Difficulties of expression were encountered in *Graham & Sibbald* v *Brash* (above). This was also one of the grounds of judgment at first instance in *Grampian Joint Police Board*. The offending words were, once again, 'the original cost of said buildings to be erected as a Police Station'. In the Lord Ordinary's view the meaning was unclear. 'Cost' might mean the cost of the materials and labour; or it might extend also to architects' and other professional fees. The ambiguity was fatal to validity. The First Division did not agree. Looking at the matter as a whole the Division was prepared to say that what was in contemplation must have been the full capital outlay of the council, and that accordingly professional fees fell to be included.[3]

Waiver and third party rights

Morrison v *Lindsay*[4] was a dispute between neighbours. A housing estate was subject to a deed of conditions in terms of which

> No dwellinghouse, garage or other building or any part thereof or any ground attached thereto shall be used for carrying on any trade or profession without the written consent of us or our successors.

The pursuer sought to prevent the defender from using her house for child-minding. At the time the action was raised no approach had been made to the superiors for consent but an approach was subsequently made and written

---

1 Though there is also authority for the contrary view. For a discussion see K G C Reid, *The Law of Property in Scotland* (1996) para 418(4). Validity is put beyond doubt by the Title Conditions (Scotland) Bill, as and when enacted, s 5 reading: 'It shall not be an objection to the validity of a real burden (whenever created) that . . . (b) an amount payable in respect of an obligation to defray, or contribute towards, some cost is not specified in the constitutive deed, if the way in which that amount can be arrived at is so specified'.

2 The two indeed overlap, for words which are unclear might become perfectly clear if extrinsic evidence is admitted.

3 2001 SC 772 at 775D: 'Since the county council had not been required to pay a capital sum for the purchase of the land, the cost of erecting the police station was, in effect, their total capital outlay in providing the facility . . . In essence, therefore, the provision was designed to ensure that, however much the property, including the police station, increased in value, the superior was not to pay the county council more than their capital outlay on the new police station. In other words, the council would not make a profit out of the transaction.'

4 Glasgow Sheriff Court, 4 October 2001, case no 2234/01 (unreported).

consent duly obtained.[1] The pursuer's interest to sue was not in doubt. As an immediate neighbour she was clearly affected by any additional disruption caused by the use of the property for a business purpose. But her title was less clear.

Usually the presence of a built-in consent facility is enough to negative any idea of *implied* right to enforce arising as between the owners on the estate. But in this case the deed of conditions gave an *express* right to enforce. In the sheriff's view that was sufficient to confer title in the present circumstances. Interim interdict was duly granted.

Fuller argument than is generally possible in an application for interim interdict would, we think, have suggested a different outcome. It is true that an express conferral of enforcement rights overrides the effect which a waiver would otherwise have in restricting enforcement rights to the superiors.[2] But it does not displace the waiver itself. The owners on the estate were given the right to enforce the deed of conditions against one another, but the deed could only be enforced according to its terms. The terms, in this particular case, were that the house was not to be used for any trade or profession without the written consent of the superiors. That consent having been given, there was no breach and hence nothing for the pursuer to enforce.

It is worth pausing to consider the effect of the abolition of the feudal system on this clause. When the feudal system is abolished, the superiors' rights will fall but those of neighbours will remain.[3] Someone in the pursuer's position will still be able to enforce the clause against someone in the defender's position. More than that, the waiver built into the clause will fly off, for there will be no superior to issue consent. The result will be to make the restriction more severe. Before feudal abolition all a person in the defender's position had to do was to get the superior's permission. After abolition such a person will have to approach all the owners on the estate.

STANDARD SECURITIES

The accessory nature of security

Trotter v *Trotter*[4] was a divorce action. The sheriff ordered, among other things, that the defender (the husband) transfer his half share in the house to the pursuer. The defender appealed various points. In particular he argued that too much had been awarded to the pursuer, that the imbalance was about £7000, and that an appropriate way of redressing the imbalance would be for the court to order the pursuer to grant to the defender a standard security over the house for that amount. It was held that the award made by the defender was justified, and the appeal was refused, but what is of some interest from a conveyancing standpoint

---

1 No formal minute of waiver was granted, but none was required in terms of the burden.
2 *Lawrence* v *Scott* 1965 SC 403.
3 Abolition of Feudal Tenure etc (Scotland) Act 2000, s 17(1).
4 2001 SLT (Sh Ct) 42.

is what was said about the proposed standard security. Sheriff Principal C G B Nicholson said:[1]

> When this matter came before myself in the course of the appeal hearing I raised a different, and more fundamental, difficulty which I have in relation to an order for the granting of a standard security in the present case. That difficulty arises from the fact that the defender's pleadings do not contain any crave for payment of a capital sum to him by the pursuer, nor do they contain any crave for an incidental order in terms of s 14(2)(k) of the Act.
>
> My difficulty, however, is not simply related to a matter of pleading. It arises from the fact that, as I understand it, any security, and in particular a standard security, must of necessity involve a debt or obligation owed by a debtor to a creditor. But, if no order is pronounced against the pursuer for payment by her of a capital sum to the defender, there is, as I see it, no way in which the relationship of debtor and creditor can be constituted with the consequence that there can be no debt which can properly be secured by the grant of a standard security.

This is a most valuable statement of principle. Security is a real right which is tied to a personal right—a debt. This makes it, in the context of real rights generally, unusual. The real right of security is said to be accessory to a personal right.[2] It is, so to speak, a parasite. The primary right is the personal right, not the real right. The personal right could exist perfectly well without the real right of security, but the converse is not true: there can be no security without a personal right to secure. Thus, suppose that Daniel borrows £100,000 from Catriona and grants her a standard security which secures that debt (plus interest accruing) and nothing else, then on the day when he pays off the last of the debt the standard security is extinguished *ipso facto*, even before any entry is made in the Land Register or Sasine Register.[3] Indeed, it is not only payment which, by ending the obligation, ends the security. Thus, in another case from 2001, *Albatown Ltd v Credential Group Ltd*,[4] a standard security was expressed as securing obligations due in terms of certain missives. The missives were superseded after two years. The effect was that the standard security ceased to secure anything and became a nullity.

Certain qualifications and exceptions exist to this general principle. One is where the security is capable of securing a fluctuating sum, such as a current account which is often in overdraft. Suppose that the account, after being overdrawn for two years, finally crawls into credit for a few days, before slipping back into overdraft again. The security is not extinguished by the fact that there was, for a few days, no secured debt. During those few days the security had a curious sort of existence: it was accessory to, or parasitic upon, a possible debt, a debt not *in esse* but *in posse*.

---

1 2001 SLT (Sh Ct) 42 at 47F–H.
2 This accessory character is also shared by cautionary obligations, and the authorities in that branch of law are thus highly relevant. For discussion see *Stair Memorial Encyclopaedia* vol 3 para 957 (Alistair Clark).
3 *Rankin v Arnot* 8 July 1680 Mor 572; *Cameron v Williamson* (1895) 22 R 293.
4 2001 GWD 27–1102 discussed at pp 62–64 above.

Although a security exists only in relation to an obligation, there is no requirement that the obligation be that of the granter of the security. The Conveyancing and Feudal Reform (Scotland) Act 1970 recognises this fact by distinguishing between the 'debtor' and the 'proprietor'. Thus, suppose that Daniel Ltd want to borrow money from Catriona and that Daniel, the main shareholder of Daniel Ltd, owns a house which can be used as collateral, either of the following two arrangements is possible:

(1) Daniel becomes a cautioner for Daniel Ltd, and grants to Catriona a standard security over his house securing his own (contingent) liability under his cautionary obligation. This is cautionary security—security for a cautionary obligation.

(2) Daniel does not become a cautioner, but grants to Catriona a standard security over his house securing the obligations of Daniel Ltd. This is third-party security— security for the obligation of a third party, and not for the obligations of the granter of the security.

Both methods are competent. In the second the granter of the security is not the debtor, and has no personal liability for the debt at all. Of course, the practical effect of the two arrangements will commonly be the same: if the debt is not paid the house will be sold. But if the debt is greater than the value of the house the practical difference becomes apparent, for in the first case Daniel remains liable for any shortfall (unless his guarantee was limited), but in the latter case he is not personally liable for a penny. The two methods are all too often not properly distinguished.

Cautionary wives

One of the bombshell cases in private law during the 1990s was *Smith* v *Bank of Scotland*,[1] in which the House of Lords held that a cautioner, or the granter of third-party security,[2] who was induced to sign by reason of misrepresentations by the principal debtor—or by reason of facility and circumvention or of undue influence—may be able to plead that fact against the creditor. The typical case is where a man has a business and the bank wants security, and the husband gets his wife to sign a standard security. In England, where the *Smith* doctrine has its roots, the term 'surety wives' has, not surprisingly, come into use. To keep the Saltire flying the term 'cautionary wives' may be used.

The question of the exact ratio of *Smith* has generated considerable discussion and some uncertainty.[3] In one of this year's cases, *Broadway* v *Clydesdale Bank plc*,[4] Lord Macfadyen helpfully sets forth at least the first part of a ratio:[5]

---

1 1997 SC(HL) 111.
2 The granter of third-party security is in a position similar to that of a cautioner. Nevertheless there are differences, as was observed above. It is curious how often the cases fail to make the distinction. Though *Smith* went all the way up to the House of Lords the question never seems to have been asked whether the standard security in that case was a cautionary standard security or a third-party security. See further the casenote to *Hewit* v *Williamson* 1998 SCLR 616.
3 For previous discussion, see *Conveyancing 1999* pp 54–56; *Conveyancing 2000* pp 86–91.
4 2001 GWD 14–552.
5 Paragraph 41 of the transcript.

Smith v *Bank of Scotland* established that a person who granted a security[1] over her property in respect of a loan made to or for the benefit of another person would be entitled, in a question with the lender, to reduction of the security if she showed (1) that her consent to the granting of the security had been improperly obtained by that other person, for example by misrepresentation or undue influence, and (2) that the lender had not acted in good faith in taking the security from her. In order to put the good faith of the lender relevantly in issue, the granter of the security would require to show that the circumstances of the case were such as to lead a reasonable lender to believe that, owing to the personal relationship between the person who benefited from the loan and the granter of the security, the consent of the latter might not be fully informed or freely given.

If the lender knows of the 'personal relationship' what steps should be taken to ensure the status of good faith? In *Smith* itself not much was said on this subject, except that the lender can meet the wife to explain the transaction and check that her consent is free and informed. But of course in practice banks have been reluctant to do this: they naturally wanted to delegate the explanation. The practice of banks has therefore been to ensure that the wife saw a solicitor before she signed. As Lord Macfadyen went on to say:[2]

> In a number of subsequent cases it has been held that if the lender knows or has reasonable cause to believe that the granter of the standard security has the benefit of legal advice in connection with the transaction, good faith does not require the lender to give the warning and advice contemplated in *Smith* (see *Forsyth*,[3] *Wright*[4] and *Etridge (No. 2)*[5]). In such circumstances the lender's good faith is adequately evidenced by his entering into the transaction in the knowledge or reasonable belief[6] that the granter of the security has the benefit of legal advice.

The *Broadway* case was covered in last year's volume when it was at debate.[7] A proof before answer was allowed and the above quotations are from this later stage of the case. Isabella Broadway, her husband Leslie, and their son Anthony were co-owners of Westquarter House, Glassford, Strathaven, the shares being ¼, ¼ and ½ respectively. Isabella and Leslie lived in one part of the house and Anthony and his wife Sandra lived in the other. There was a family business called John Gardiner Environmental Services Ltd. At the start of 1992 the shareholdings were Isabella 16.33%, Leslie 51.04% and Anthony 32.63% respectively. Isabella and Anthony were directors, but Leslie had retired. In 1992 it was decided that Anthony and Sandra would put in a large amount of capital

---

1 We would add that an unsecured guarantee would also be covered by the *Smith* doctrine.
2 Paragraph 43 of the transcript.
3 *Forsyth* v *Royal Bank of Scotland* 2000 SLT 1295.
4 *Wright* v *Cotias Investments Inc* 2001 SLT 353.
5 *Royal Bank of Scotland* v *Etridge (No. 2)* [1998] 4 All ER 705 (CA). This case has since been partly upheld and partly reversed by the House of Lords. See below.
6 Thus, even if the wife did not actually see a solicitor, the bank is protected if it reasonably thought that she did. As Lord Macfadyen says: 'What matters is the defenders' knowledge or reasonable belief that the pursuer had a solicitor acting for her in the matter, not whether she actually received from that solicitor appropriate advice about the risks of the transaction.'
7 *Conveyancing 2000* pp 87–88.

in return for a new issue of shares in their favour. This was duly done. Because Anthony and Sandra did not have sufficient available funds themselves they borrowed £200,000 from the Clydesdale Bank. The bank wanted security for the loan, and the three co-owners of the house granted a standard security. It is not clear whether (from the standpoint of Isabella and Leslie) this was third-party security, or whether they also personally guaranteed the loan, but it rather appears as if the former was the case. Later, problems developed and the bank sought to enforce their security. Isabella argued that she had signed by reason of the undue influence of her son or her husband or both.[1] She sought reduction of the standard security in so far as it affected her quarter share of the house. She was unsuccessful. It was held that the bank had reasonable grounds for believing that she was receiving independent legal advice. Her case also failed on two other grounds. She had not proved undue influence or that, had it not been for such influence, she would not have signed.

Given the findings in fact, the pursuer's case could not succeed. But the opinion of Lord Macfadyen contains a valuable analysis of the law, including— though we have not touched on this—a valuable analysis of the law of undue influence. It is also noteworthy that his Lordship warned against 'undue reliance on the categorisation developed in the English authorities'. Anyone who has studied the labyrinthine and sometimes most strange[2] English rules in this area will welcome that statement.

One of the cases mentioned by Lord Macfadyen was *Royal Bank of Scotland* v *Etridge (No 2)*, which has been grinding its way through the English courts for many years and which was finally heard, together with a set of similar cases, by the House of Lords in 2001.[3] Whilst the *Smith* doctrine is not identical with the corresponding English doctrine, it was evolved out of it, and it is inevitable that *Etridge* will have an influence north of the border.

Etridge confirms the basic principles set forth in the landmark decision of *Barclays Bank* v *O'Brien*,[4] the case out of which the *Smith* doctrine emerged. It has a good deal to say about the duties of the solicitor who advises the surety wife. It slightly tones down what had been said about this in the Court of Appeal,[5] where quite impossibly onerous standards were imposed, standards that no solicitor, however competent and conscientious, could ever meet. But the standards set by the House of Lords are still demanding. The following is a (not necessarily complete) summary.[6] The solicitor who sees the surety wife should:

---

1 So this was a case of a cautionary wife and mother. By the time of the action Leslie seems to have died.
2 Such as the doctrine of 'presumed undue influence'.
3 [2001] 4 All ER 449.
4 [1994] 1 AC 180.
5 For discussion of the Court of Appeal decision in *Etridge* see G L Gretton, 'Good News for Bankers—Bad News for Lawyers?' 1999 SLT (News) 53. One duty imposed by the Court of Appeal which does not seem to be repeated in the House of Lords is the duty to 'probe the stability of the marriage'.
6 The report is massive, running to about 55,000 words, and hence far from easy to summarise.

- Explain why the solicitor is involved. This should include an explanation that if the surety wife in future seeks to reduce the deed the bank would be likely to rely on the present meeting.

- Satisfy him/herself that the surety wife wishes the solicitor to advise her.

- Satisfy him/herself that there is no conflict of interest.

- Explain the nature of the documents and what their legal effect will be.

- Explain that there is a risk.

- Obtain from the bank detailed information including copies of all important documents, such as the husband's loan application form.

- State what debts are involved and their amount, and indicate the main features of the loan.

- Explain that the amounts and terms may change and that it may be that that will happen without further reference to the surety wife.

- Discuss with her her own financial means and the means of her husband.

- Explain that she has a choice and check that she really does wish to proceed.

- Check that she wishes the firm to write to the bank confirming that she had been given independent legal advice.

All this should be done in the absence of the husband, and in non-technical language. The firm is not barred from acting merely because it also acts for the husband or for the bank, but it must be satisfied that there is no conflict of interest.

If these standards also apply in Scots law—which is highly likely—then any firm of solicitors must think carefully before advising a cautionary wife. When the bank enforces the security, what will she do? She is likely to have no defence against the bank, because the bank can play its trump: 'but you saw a solicitor before you signed'. If she is still living with her husband she may not want to sue him, and whether she is living with him or not it is likely that he is insolvent anyway—for otherwise the bank would probably not have enforced their security. So she sues the firm who advised her. Somewhere in the long list of duties given above there may be something she can claim was not properly done. It will be noted that the advice which must be tendered is not only legal advice. A solicitor is qualified to explain the legal nature and effect of legal documents, and to form an impression of whether consent has been given in a free and informed manner. But the House of Lords seems to expect the solicitor to go far beyond that, and act as a financial consultant. Many will feel that the standards set are unacceptable.

Of course, to obtain damages against the law firm it is not enough to show that the firm failed in its duties. The cautionary wife would also have to satisfy the 'but for' test—to show that had it not been for the law firm's failure to advise her properly she never would have signed. That is not an easy hurdle to get over—as was illustrated by the *Broadway* case (above).

It should be added that in *Etridge* the House of Lords also sets out in some detail the duties incumbent on the bank. For instance the bank must write to the wife explaining that the bank will require her to see a solicitor, and why. It must ask her to nominate a solicitor, and should say that she is free to use the same solicitor as her husband. It must provide all necessary information, including if necessary copy documents, to the solicitor. Finally, the House of Lords seems to be saying that the principle that a lender is 'put on its inquiry' will now apply to *all* cases where the relationship between the principal debtor and the guarantor is a non-commercial one.[1] This, of itself, might prove a significant extension of the *O'Brien/Smith* doctrines.

Disputing default

There were two cases this year in which the creditor in enforcing a standard security argued that it was not competent to dispute default: *J Sykes & Sons (Fish Merchants) Ltd* v *Grieve*[2] and *Gardiner* v *Jacques Vert plc*.[3]

In *Sykes*, James Watt Grieve and Georgina Rosa Grieve granted a form A standard security to the pursuers for a sum of £20,000. Later the pursuers served a calling-up notice, and subsequently raised an action seeking declarator of their rights, authority to sell, etc. The defenders pled that no sum had in fact ever been advanced to them by the pursuers, notwithstanding the terms of the standard security. Instead, the pursuers had made advances to a company called Spurbranch Ltd. The defenders counterclaimed for the pursuers to be ordained to grant a discharge of the standard security. The question before the court was whether a proof should be allowed as to the defenders' averments or whether summary decree should be granted. It was held that the defenders were entitled to a proof before answer. The pursuers argued that terms of the standard security, acknowledging indebtedness, should be regarded as conclusive. This argument was rejected. The pursuers also argued that since the defenders had done nothing to challenge the validity of the calling-up notices they were now precluded from disputing the sums set forth in those notices. This argument too was rejected.

There can be little doubt that this decision is correct. It is obvious that, standing the terms of the standard security, the defenders would have an uphill battle. The burden would be on them to prove that nothing had been advanced, and to satisfy the court why it was that they had signed an untrue admission of indebtedness. But it could not be said in advance that the defence was so weak or unstateable as to justify the court in granting summary decree. One might add that article 6 of the European Convention on Human Rights means that summary decree procedure can be used only in the clearest cases, though it does not seem that this point was argued in *Sykes* itself.

In *Gardiner*, John Gardiner ran a fashion business known as 'Gardiner Fashion Group' trading from a warehouse at 74 Miller Street, Glasgow, and a fashion

---

1 And the fact that the principal debtor is a company and the wife is herself a director is expressly said not to be relevant: even in such a case the bank is 'put on its inquiry'.
2 2001 GWD 23–866.
3 2001 GWD 38–1433 rev 2002 GWD 5–167.

shop called 'Vanity Fair' at 42 New Kirk Road, Bearsden. It appears that he was a sole trader. He had a contract with Jacques Vert plc whereby he was the sole distributor of the latter's goods in Scotland. As is common in such cases, goods were delivered to Gardiner on a credit basis. Because of possible credit risk, the company asked for security, and standard securities were granted over the shop and also Gardiner's home at 6 Thorn Drive, Bearsden. Since the latter was co-owned with his wife Sheena, she also signed this latter security.

Things began to go wrong, and in May 2001 the company raised an action against Gardiner, alleging breach of contract. Gardiner denied that he was in breach, asserted that the company itself was in breach, and counterclaimed for damages. On 8 June 2001 the company served a certificate as to the alleged indebtedness of Gardiner:

I, Paul Allen, being a duly appointed Director of Jacques Vert plc, a company incorporated under the Companies Acts and having its Registered Office formerly at 23 Plumbers Row, London, and now at 22 Plumbers Row, London (the 'Company') hereby certify that as at the date hereof the total amount of principal due by you to the Company is £136,572.76 made up as under-noted. Interest at the rate of 9.25% per annum is due on the total amount of principal from and after the date of this Certificate.

Yours faithfully,

Paul Allen (Mr. P. Allen)

Date: 8 June 2001

Note referred to:-

M Season Order	£2,979.17
P Season Order	£129,856.89
Special Account	£676.80
Sample Account	£3,059.90
Total amount of principal due	**£136,572.76**

Four days later, sheriff officers served calling-up notices upon the Gardiners for both standard securities. The notice in respect of the shop was as follows:

TAKE NOTICE that JACQUES VERT plc . . . requires payment of the principal sum of one hundred and thirty six thousand five hundred and seventy two pounds and seventy six pence (£136,527.76) with interest thereon at the rate of 9.25% per annum from the Eighth day of June Two Thousand and One (subject to such amendment of the principal sum and the amount of interest as may subsequently be determined) secured by a Standard Security by you in favour of the said Jacques Vert plc registered under Title Number DMB 2046 on Twenty sixth June Two Thousand; And that failing full payment of the said sum and interest thereon and expenses within two months after the date of service of this demand, the subjects of the security may be sold.

The two notices (to both Gardiners) in respect of the house were in similar terms.

The Gardiners responded by petitioning the Court of Session to suspend the operation of these calling-up notices, and for interim suspension. Since such petitions are not common, the wording may be of interest:

> To suspend the certificate served upon the petitioner on 8 June 2001 and the calling-up notice served on him on 12 June 2001; and to suspend the said certificate and calling-up notice *ad interim* . . .

At first instance interim suspension was granted by Lady Cosgrove.[1] She observed that there was a discrepancy in the calling-up notices, in that the sum in words and the sum in figures were different, albeit only by a modest amount. Although she made no decision on the point, she remarked that:[2]

> It may be that such an error raises serious doubts about the validity of the calling-up notices. A high degree of accuracy is required where any party uses any form of diligence or summary measure.

In the second place, she said that since 'I could not see, in the contractual documents before me, any provision (such as is often found in bank and other loans) that the creditor's certificate would in itself be sufficient or conclusive proof of the debt due' it followed that the debtor was entitled to dispute the figure stated in the certificate. This statement merits two cheers although not three. In fact it seems unlikely that 'conclusivity clauses' take effect according to their terms. The law does not permit a creditor to have the power to state what is due, without any right in the debtor to question the figure stated. Instead, such clauses merely raise a *presumption* that the figure stated is correct. This was probably always the law of Scotland, but today to construe a conclusivity clause literally would be to deny the debtor the right to a fair hearing which is guaranteed by the sixth article of the European Convention on Human Rights.[3]

The respondents reclaimed and the interim order was recalled by an Extra Division of the Inner House.[4] The point about the discrepancy as to the sum claimed was passed over in silence, perhaps as a matter of concession by counsel.[5] So it is uncertain what the Division might have said on this point. The reason for the decision seems to have been that the petitioner's pleadings did not set forth a stateable case for saying that the sum in the calling-up notice was not

---

1 2001 GWD 38–1433.
2 Paragraph 40 of the transcript.
3 The subject is too large to be entered into here. To the statement of the law given in the text there exist certain qualifications, such as pay-first-argue-later arrangements, and 'abstract' payment obligations in international trade such as documentary credits and first-demand bonds.
4 2002 GWD 5–167.
5 At para 6 of the transcript Lord Cameron of Lochbroom, giving the opinion of the court, said that 'counsel did not suggest that *ex facie* the calling-up notices . . . there was any defect by way of want of form or the like'.

due. The competency of the petitioner's attack on the calling-up notice was not, however, questioned.

Behind *Sykes* and *Gardiner* there is a wider issue. The current law does not require of a person who wishes to enforce a standard security that there must first be established the existence of the debt and the fact of default by means of an action for payment. Whilst heritable creditors usually do raise an action, in principle it is possible to enforce a standard security by sale without any court process whatsoever. In that case if the debtor wishes to dispute the creditor's rights there exists no process to do so and he or she must take the initiative with a separate action of, for instance, suspension. To require the creditor to constitute the debt would, it may be argued, be no more than justice to the debtor, and could also lead to a simplification of procedure. It would mean that in cases such as *Gardiner* or *Sykes* the core issues could be heard and determined in the form of action which is designed for such disputes—an action for payment. That quite complex questions of fact and law should have to be shunted off into a suspension petition is hardly satisfactory, not to mention the point that the effect is to reverse the burden of proof.

VARIATION AND DISCHARGE OF LAND OBLIGATIONS

Remote superiors

Quite often superiors own no land in the vicinity of the feus. They are, in other words, 'remote' superiors. Curiously, it has never been decided whether remote superiors are able to enforce the burdens in their charters. The difficulty, from the superiors' point of view, is interest to enforce. It is true that, formally speaking, interest is presumed, but that is a matter of onus of proof; and if the only real interest is the prospect of income from minutes of waiver, this may not be an interest which the law is willing to protect.[1] Whether that is really so is, however, unclear and, with feudal abolition imminent, may become no more than an uncertain question in legal history. Certainly remote superiors are given short shrift by the Abolition of Feudal Tenure etc (Scotland) Act 2000, for real burdens can be preserved only by those who own property in the neighbourhood.

But even if remote superiors have interest to enforce in the technical sense, they are probably unable to resist an application to the Lands Tribunal for variation and discharge. That point is usefully emphasised in *Moran's Exrs* v *Shenstone Properties Ltd*.[2] Mrs Moran owned a house at 67 Coillesdene Avenue, Edinburgh. In 1997 she conveyed part of the site to her son and daughter-in-law

1 J M Halliday, *The Conveyancing and Feudal Reform (Scotland) Act 1970* (2nd edn, 1977) p 41; K G C Reid, *The Law of Property in Scotland* (1996) para 408. The issue is touched upon in another recent decision of the Lands Tribunal, *Strathclyde Joint Police Board* v *The Elderslie Estates* 2001 GWD 27–1101.

2 2001 Hous LR 124. The Tribunal comprised Mr A R MacLeary FRICS. For an earlier case see *Harris* v *Douglas* 1993 SLT (Lands Tr) 56.

who proceeded to build a second house. But while planning permission had been obtained, no one, it seems, had thought to obtain the superiors' consent, as was required in terms of a feu charter of 1936. As so often, matters came to light only when the house[1] came to be sold, by Mrs Moran's executors. On being approached for a minute of waiver, the superiors asked for £7,500, later negotiated down to £5,000. With disarming candour they explained that the 'premium ... will be based on 15 per cent of the net development gain, in accordance with standard practice'. Faced with this demand, a joint application to the Lands Tribunal was made by the executors and the purchasers.[2]

Although opposed by the superiors the application was readily granted. Three alternative grounds for variation or discharge are set out in the 1970 Act,[3] and the application turned on the second of these, which invites the Tribunal to weigh burden and benefit. Discharge may be awarded if 'the obligation is unduly burdensome compared with any benefit resulting or which would result from its performance'. In the case of a remote superior there is unlikely to be any benefit to counterbalance the burden imposed on the vassal. The superior's property is not affected one way or another by whether the burden survives or is discharged. Rather there is only personal benefit from the hope of waiver income, and that is not the kind of benefit that is recognised under the 1970 Act. Discharge will therefore be granted. The Tribunal put it this way:[4]

> The superiors in this case, while contending that the obligation is not unduly burdensome, do not claim any benefit to themselves from its continuing observance; and, it is exclusively from the points of view of the burdened and benefited properties that the terms of para (b) have to be considered. Indeed, it is abundantly clear that had the applicants been willing to pay a sufficiently large sum to them the superiors would have given their permission for a house to be built on the subjects. Hence the tribunal concludes that they derive no *legitimate*[5] benefit from the performance of the obligation.
>
> It is not incumbent on a burdened proprietor to show that the obligation has become more burdensome than it originally was if it can be shown that, in comparison with the burden imposed on him, there is little or no benefit to the superior in continuing to be allowed to enforce it. That is clearly the case here.

Two words of caution are necessary. First, the position is sometimes complicated by co-feuars' rights. It should not be assumed without inquiry that the superior is the only person with title to enforce. If neighbours can enforce as well as the superior, then any argument based on remoteness is useless.

---

1 In this case the original house.
2 In accordance with its usual practice the Tribunal disregarded the fact that the burden had already been breached, so that the application was considered 'on the assumption that the house has not been built' (para 16–18).
3 Conveyancing and Feudal Reform (Scotland) Act 1970, s 1(3). Often the Tribunal considers more than one ground. In the present case the application succeeded both on the second ground (discussed in the text) and also on the third.
4 At paras 16–20 and 16–21.
5 Our emphasis.

Second, even if a discharge is granted by the Tribunal, the superiors may be entitled to compensation. In practice, however, this will seldom be awarded. The 1970 Act allows compensation on two alternative grounds.[1] One is in respect of any substantial loss or disadvantage suffered by the proprietor as such benefited proprietor in consequence of the variation or discharge. This is interpreted by the Tribunal as excluding compensation for loss of income from minutes of waiver, an approach affirmed in *Strathclyde Joint Police Board* v *The Elderslie Estates Ltd* (another new case involving remote superiors).[2] In that case it was argued, unsuccessfully, that such an interpretation was contrary to the European Convention on Human Rights.[3] The overall effect is to exclude claims under this head from remote superiors.

The other ground for compensation is to make up for any reduction in consideration consequent on the imposition of the burden. Such a reduction might affect either feuduty or the price (grassum). Usually neither can be shown. In this respect *Moran's Exrs* is typical. Notwithstanding an elaborate argument by the superiors, the Tribunal was not persuaded that there had been any reduction in feuduty at the time the burden was imposed, in 1937.

Determining reasonable use

The third (and most popular) ground on which variation or discharge may be granted is where 'the existence of the obligation impedes some reasonable use of the land'.[4] The question of how reasonableness is to be assessed was considered in *Itelsor Ltd* v *Smith*.[5] The sheer ordinariness of the facts makes this a decision of some significance.

12 Harefield Road, Dundee was a derelict site of around 0.25 hectares. A disposition of 1924 restricted development to a single house. When the owners applied to have the restriction removed, the initial response of the Tribunal was to continue the application pending the grant of planning permission. The Tribunal was reluctant to discharge the restriction in the absence of detailed proposals for development. That would be a blank cheque:[6]

> We do not consider it safe or prudent to permit discharge of the obligation for unspecified residential use where this degree of uncertainty remains [ie as to its scope and hence its reasonableness]. Nor do we consider it to be appropriate for this Tribunal to lay down arbitrary criteria in respect of the type of development, or number of houses, to be permitted without having regard to the many technical issues which may critically affect the design and layout of a site such as this. It is incumbent upon the applicants to demonstrate that their proposed use of the subjects is reasonable. This they have been unable to do to a sufficient level of confidence. It is just for this reason that, while planning permission is not a prerequisite for a decision

1 Conveyancing and Feudal Reform (Scotland) Act 1970, s 1(4).
2 2002 SLT (Lands Tr) 2.
3 For a discussion, see pp 35–36 above.
4 Conveyancing and Feudal Reform (Scotland) Act 1970, s 1(3)(c).
5 2001 Hous LR 120. The Tribunal comprised Mr A R MacLeary FRICS.
6 Para 15–21.

on such a matter by the Tribunal, it is nevertheless usually offered as evidence of the reasonableness of a proposal when an application is made.

Planning permission was important for another reason also. Once permission was granted (for four houses and two flats), the Tribunal was absolved from considering such matters as local amenity or the possible need for houses in the area. These were properly matters for the planning authority and not for the Tribunal.[1] In evaluating the reasonableness of the proposed use the Tribunal would confine its attention to the amenity of the immediate neighbours, and in particular of those benefited proprietors whom the restriction was designed to protect. This is a further sign of a gradual retreat from public law to private law on the part of the Tribunal.[2] The retreat is indeed logical, for if real burdens exist to protect private amenity, it is with such amenity that the Tribunal is primarily concerned. As and when the Title Conditions (Scotland) Bill is enacted, the retreat will become a rout, for the Tribunal will no longer be required to consider reasonableness of use at all. Use will merely be one of a number of factors used to assess the overall reasonableness of discharge, and it will be enough under this head if the use is in fact impeded by the condition in question.[3]

On the particular facts in *Itelsor* the Tribunal had little difficulty in concluding that the proposed use was reasonable in the limited sense in which that concept was being employed:[4]

> While the development is relatively dense it is in the nature of a cul-de-sac development of the kind normally referred to as 'quiet'. There is no doubt that there will be some breach of privacy to the objectors as neighbours, but that privacy would have been breached in any case with the use of the subjects as residential development even with the one or two houses they would prefer to see there. Because of the arrangement of the houses on the site the effect on their privacy will be kept to a minimum. They will not be overlooked in any obvious or potentially intrusive way and most of the mass of the development will be screened from them.

SOLICITORS AND ESTATE AGENTS

Prescription as a defence to negligence claims

Britannia Building Society v *Clarke*[5] is a decision of some importance as to prescription as a defence to actions of negligence against law firms by lending institutions.

---

1 Paras 15–33 and 15–34.
2 For an earlier case, see *T & I Consultants* v *Cullion* 1998 Hous LR 9. And see also Sir Crispin Agnew of Lochnaw, *Variation and Discharge of Land Obligations* (1999) pp 116–117.
3 Title Conditions (Scotland) Bill, s 94. For an explanation of the change, see Scottish Law Commission, *Discussion Paper on Real Burdens* (Scot Law Com DP No 106, 1998) paras 6.43—6.45; Scottish Law Commission, *Report on Real Burdens* (Scot Law Com No 181, 2000; available on www.scotlawcom.gov.uk) para 6.76.
4 Para 15–31.
5 2001 GWD 18–710.

In 1989 the pursuers provided secured finance for the purchasers of several cottages at Cowiefaulds Cottages, Gateside, Fife. In each case the same firm of solicitors acted for the building society. The purchasers soon defaulted and the securities had to be enforced by sale, the sales taking place in 1991 and 1992. The pursuers suffered loss. In 2000 they raised an action against the law firm in question. They alleged that the firm had withheld information which, had it been known to them, would have meant that the loans would never have been made. It is not altogether clear from the opinion of the Lord Ordinary just what the defenders are supposed to have done wrong, but there is some suggestion that the purchasers were all employees of the seller, and that the law firm concerned may have known this. Whether or not the pursuers could have made anything of this we do not know, for, not surprisingly, the defenders pled the quinquennial prescription.

To counter this defence, the pursuers sought to rely on s 11(3) of the Prescription and Limitation (Scotland) Act 1973. That says that if 'the creditor was not aware, and could not with reasonable diligence have been aware, that loss, injury or damage caused as aforesaid had occurred' then the quinquennium runs from 'the date when the creditor first became, or could with reasonable diligence have become, so aware'. The pursuers argued that it was not until their files were examined by new solicitors acting for them in 1996 that they were able to become aware of the alleged wrong done to them. This argument failed at debate, it being held that, even without proof, the pleadings had nothing to support a possible conclusion that the requirements of s 11(3) had been satisfied. The Lord Ordinary (Macfadyen) commented:[1]

> I am of opinion that it is incumbent on the pursuers, who are after all a lending institution well accustomed to such transactions, to explain why it is that they did nothing until 1996 . . . Their averments contain nothing to explain why the steps which they chose to take in 1996 could not with reasonable diligence have been undertaken earlier. I am therefore of opinion that this is a case in which a bare averment that the pursuers could not with reasonable diligence have become aware earlier that they had a claim does not constitute a relevant invocation of section 11(3). To make a relevant case the pursuers would, in my opinion, have had to set out facts and circumstances explaining why they could not, with reasonable diligence, have discovered earlier than 1996 that they had suffered loss due to an act, neglect or default.

This decision is commonsensical and will be welcomed. It should, however, be noted that an element in the decision was the fact that the pursuers were in the business of secured lending. They were, to use sociological jargon, 'repeat players'. A commercially unsophisticated client, by contrast, would have a better chance of successfully pleading the s 11(3) argument.

The next two cases also involve prescription as a defence.[2]

---

1 Paragraph 19 of the transcript.
2 And see also *Cole v Lonie* 2001 SC 610 (digested above at pp 4–5).

A duty to advise on tax consequences?

Smith v *Gordon & Smyth*[1] raises the question of whether a solicitor has a duty to give tax planning advice to a client who is selling heritable property.

John Smith owned Back Priestfield Farm. He sold part of it for development for the sum of £965,000 and thereby incurred liability of £868,482 for Capital Gains Tax. He could have obtained roll-over relief by investing the proceeds of sale. In fact only part of the proceeds were reinvested, by purchasing another farm, Turnlaw Farm, but even this partial benefit was reduced because title was taken not in his sole name but in joint names with his wife. Later he raised an action against (i) his solicitors (ii) his original accountants and (iii) his subsequent accountants for having failed to give him proper tax advice. His claim was for lost roll-over relief of £167,092 plus certain other alleged losses, bringing the total amount to £245,000. The claim against the defenders was joint and several. A number of points came up for decision at the preliminary debate on the pleadings.

One defence advanced by the law firm was that they had no duty to advise their client about tax implications (unless specifically asked to do so) since he was employing accountants. Lady Paton, allowing proof before answer, said:[2]

> It is possible that a professional adviser may have an obligation to give a client advice about a particular matter despite the fact that the client also has the services of another professional adviser. I am unable to conclude at this stage, without hearing evidence, that no duty rests upon a solicitor to give any advice about the possible tax consequences of a conveyancing transaction because the solicitor is aware that the client has the services of an accountant.

Following *Grunwald* v *Hughes*[3] it was held that the three defenders would indeed be liable jointly and severally, if the pursuer could prove his averments.

The defenders pled prescription. It was held, in conformity with s 11(2) of the Prescription and Limitation (Scotland) Act 1973, that since any duty to give tax advice was an ongoing one and not a duty which existed solely at the moment of the sale:[4]

> Any alleged failure on the part of the first defenders [the solicitors] to fulfil such an obligation—in other words, any alleged 'neglect or default' on their part—would in my view be a continuous neglect or default, lasting until 28 November 1994, after which date the pursuer could no longer claim roll-over relief.

It followed that the pursuer's claim had not prescribed.

The first of these issues (duty to advise about tax implications) is of particular concern to conveyancers. The decision to leave the matter to proof is understandable, but it would have been helpful to give some guidance as to what at least are the presumptive duties of solicitors in such a case. It is arguable that

---

1 2001 GWD 26–1066.
2 Paragraph 76 of the transcript.
3 1965 SLT 209.
4 Paragraph 84 of the transcript.

in such circumstances solicitors are presumptively under no obligation to give tax advice. At all events, the practical lesson, as ever, is that the clients should either be given tax advice (assuming that the law firm is able to do so satisfactorily) or be informed that they should obtain separate tax advice.

One final point. The pursuer averred that Turnlaw Farm had been put into joint names without his consent. It is not clear what actually happened in this particular case. But it is worth mentioning that this is a matter which all too often goes wrong. It is easy to regard the husband and wife as a sort of single unit, so that it is a rather minor matter whether title is taken (or missives concluded) in the name of husband or wife or both. Instructions—and changes of instructions—are often taken from just one of the spouses. Often nothing is recorded or confirmed. Under pressures of time this is understandable but it is nevertheless both wrong and unwise. Another of this year's cases, *G W Tait & Sons* v *Taylor* (below) points up the same general moral. It should be added that in Scots law it is possible for a person to buy land without ever signing anything, a remarkable fact which itself facilitates muddles.

Paying out and claiming back

The facts of *G W Tait & Sons* v *Taylor*[1] are unusual and striking. In August 1991 a Mr Ronald Andrew Taylor, acting through his solicitors Messrs G W Tait & Sons, concluded missives to buy a house at 3 Belford Mews, Edinburgh, the seller being a Mr John R Thomson. The price was £130,000. At the same time Mr Taylor arranged to borrow £123,500 with the North of England Building Society, to be secured on the property. The missives provided, as usual, that the disposition would be granted to the purchaser or his nominees. After missives were concluded, Mr Taylor instructed his solicitors to take title in the joint names of himself and his wife, Susan. The engrossed disposition, in favour of both Taylors, was duly sent to Mr Thomson's solicitors, and Mr Thomson duly signed it. The mechanics of settlement are a little unclear, but it seems that the disposition was delivered to Mr Taylor's solicitors on 21 August and the price was paid on 23 August. At this stage the building society loan had not yet been paid over, so that the price was obtained on the basis of bridging finance. On 27 August Mr Taylor signed the standard security in favour of the building society, and the same day the loan cheque was requisitioned, and soon received.

The difficulty will be at once apparent. The disposition was to Mr and Mrs Taylor, but the loan agreement was only with Mr Taylor, and the standard security was signed only by Mr Taylor. The most natural way to put this problem right would have been to prepare a joint standard security, asking Mrs Taylor to sign, and asking the building society to confirm that they would have no objection.[2] Whether this solution was attempted, and, if so, why it did not take place, does not emerge from the opinion of the Lord Ordinary (Dawson).

---

1 2001 GWD 33–1320.
2 Presumably the latter would not have been a problem since a joint and several loan to two people is obviously more secure than a loan to just one of them.

What happened to the disposition and standard security is not wholly clear. It seems, however, that the disposition was never recorded, but that the standard security was recorded in the Register of Sasines on 15 May 1992. We return to the question of the title later.

Beginning in September 1992, Mr Taylor's solicitors began to press the seller, Mr Thomson, to sign a new disposition, in favour of Mr Taylor alone. It does not appear that these requests were authorised by either Mr or Mrs Taylor. Mr Thomson refused. One can understand why. To grant a disposition to A and B, and later, without B's consent, and without judicial authority, to grant a disposition just to A, would be a remarkable proceeding. If it was acceptable to Mrs Taylor, why did she not authorise it? If it was not acceptable to Mrs Taylor, compliance with the request would have created the possibility of a damages action at her instance. Mr Thomson sat on his hands.

In the meantime, the building society were not receiving monthly payments. Late in 1992 they decide to enforce their standard security. They then discovered that the standard security could not be enforced, because title was still vested in the seller. Moreover, Mr Taylor had vanished and no assets of his could be found. So the loan was a total loss. In 1994 they sued Messrs G W Tait & Sons for damages, and eventually in 1996 settlement was reached at a figure of £152,500. In return the building society assigned to Messrs G W Tait & Sons all rights which they had or might have against Mr and Mrs Taylor. In the meantime, in 1995, Mr Taylor was sequestrated.

Having paid damages to the building society, Messrs G W Tait & Sons sought to recover their loss from Mrs Taylor and Mr Thomson, and sued them when they declined to pay. The pursuers took the view that Mrs Taylor, who had been living in the property since settlement, should have been paying rent to them. Since they were not the landlords the logic is unclear, but we quote the Lord Ordinary:

> They further aver that she has been able to live in the subjects since August 1991 without paying rent. They therefore claim rent in respect of that right of occupation of the sum of £76,824 being the sum first sued for, plus a payment of £900 per calendar month from 1 July 2000 onwards.

The balance of their loss should be met, the pursuers argued, by the seller, Mr Thomson. The claim was said to be based on the law of unjustified enrichment. The general idea was that the pursuers had suffered a loss and that the defenders had allegedly enjoyed a windfall gain, effectively at the expense of the pursuers.

The starting point of the pursuers' case was that the disposition which they had drafted was, as they put it, 'mistaken', and the reason that it was 'mistaken' was that 'the loan was secured by the standard security which had been granted by Mr Taylor alone'. The logic is difficult to follow. In the words of the Lord Ordinary:[1]

---

1 Paragraph 4 of the transcript.

In terms of their own pleadings that averment cannot be correct. As at 16 August when they claim to have made an error in respect of the 'overlooking' of something in the standard security, that document had not even been executed. Not until 27 August, that is to say after the purchase transaction had been completed, was the standard security executed. It is plain that there was nothing 'mistaken' about the disposition. The pursuers had complied with their clients' instructions in taking the title in names of himself and his wife.[1] The seller had complied with his obligation in the missives to grant title in the name of Mr Taylor 'or his nominee'. Thus at settlement on 23 August no 'error' had been made in so far as the purchase transaction was concerned. That was conducted perfectly properly and was by that date completed. The title 'mistaken disposition' is therefore, quite clearly, an erroneous description.

Building on this weak foundation, the pursuers argued that Mrs Taylor had been enriched at their expense by living in the property, and that Mr Thomson had been enriched at their expense by having been paid the purchase price. The logic is not easy to follow. Since she was one of the disponees, it would seem that Mrs Taylor had the right to live in the house without paying anyone anything, least of all the pursuers. Likewise, Mr Thomson had simply been paid the price to which he was, as seller, fully entitled. At some stage during the case the claim against Mr Thomson was, it seems, abandoned, but the claim against Mrs Taylor was pursued. The Lord Ordinary, unsurprisingly, dismissed the action.

In attempting to state a relevant claim, the pursuers invoked a branch of the law of unjustified enrichment known as the *actio de in rem verso*. The Lord Ordinary took the view that this is not part of Scots law, the basis for this being mainly the fact that the 10th edition of Gloag & Henderson *The Law of Scotland* does not mention it, the chapter of that work on unjustified enrichment having been written by Lord Rodger of Earlsferry.[2] As to whether this is right in law we will express no view. But we would suggest that in any event the *actio de in rem verso* would not have supported the claims of the pursuers.

A number of further points deserve mention. One of the defences was prescription, the action not having been begun until 1999. It was held that even if the claim had been well founded in law, which it was not, it would have failed because of prescription. The pursuers sought to rely on Sched 1 para 2(c) to the Prescription and Limitation (Scotland) Act 1973, which says that obligations 'relating to land' are not subject to the quinquennial prescription. It is often rather unclear when para 2(c) does and does not apply, and no doubt in some vague sense the action in question did have some connection with land, since it had its roots in a conveyancing transaction. The Lord Ordinary rejected, surely rightly, this attempt to push the boundaries of para 2(c) over the horizon.

---

1 We would comment here that to take title in joint names requires the consent of *both* persons in question. Mr Taylor so consented, but did Mrs Taylor? We presume she did, but the details of how and when are obscure, as is the connected question of whether the pursuers at any stage were acting on her behalf.

2 Since the case was argued the 11th edition (2001) has been published. Lord Rodger is no longer one of the credited authors.

Next, we return to the question of the title. As has been said, it seems that the pursuers recorded the standard security but not the disposition. Since title remained with the seller, Mr Thomson, the standard security was void, though it was presumably capable of being validated by accretion had the title of the granter, Mr Taylor, later been completed. It rather appears that the disposition remained in the repositories of the pursuers. Had the disposition been recorded the lenders would at least have obtained a valid security over a one-half share of the property, so that when the wreck came something could have been salvaged. We understand that at some stage after the action had been commenced Mrs Taylor recorded in the Register of Sasines a notice of title to her half share, deducing title through the unrecorded disposition.[1]

One curious aspect of the story is the position of Mr Taylor's trustee in sequestration, who may have had a claim to Mr Taylor's half share, and possibly also a claim against Mrs Taylor if her half share could be regarded as having been based on a gratuitous alienation.[2] But these issues take us outwith the context of this particular litigation, and we do not seek to explore them.

REGISTRATION OF TITLE

Possession and dispossession

In *Tesco Stores Ltd* v *Keeper of the Registers of Scotland*[3] Safeway acquired property at Lonend, Paisley, their title being registered on 8 October 1997 under title number REN 56654. This was not a first registration: the title on the Land Register dated from 1984. At that time the southern boundary of the property, at a particular point, was the mid-line of a river, the White Cart Water. Shortly before Safeway's acquisition, however, this boundary was altered on the title plan so that it came to extend some two metres beyond the mid-line. The alteration was carried out at the Registers as part of the digital conversion of the map base and without reference to any of the owners. It was both mistaken and, for some time, unnoticed. In acquiring the property, Safeway were unaware of the new boundary to the south.

The new area thus added to title number REN 56654 was previously held on a Sasine title,[4] and later in the same year the whole land held under that title

---

1 The style notice of title in the Conveyancing (Scotland) Act 1924 (Sched B Form 1) expects the solicitor to certify: 'Which last recorded title and subsequent writ (or writs) have been presented to me . . .' This raises questions of who owned the disposition (presumably Mrs Taylor and her husband, or his trustee in sequestration), who had custody of it, whether there was a valid lien over it, who had access to it, whether title is deducible through a copy deed (see note 6 of Sched B), the possible role of proving the tenor, and so on. We cannot enter into these questions here.
2 The Lord Ordinary said: 'If her share had been a gift from Mr Taylor, which can be presumed as Mrs Taylor was his wife, there is no reason why she should not retain it.' But this remark was made in the context of the litigation and probably was not intended to have reference to the possible rights of the trustee in sequestration.
3 2001 SLT (Lands Tr) 23. The Tribunal comprised Lord McGhie and A R MacLeary FRICS.
4 In fact that title was itself invalid as proceeding on an *a non domino* conveyance which had not been followed by possession for the period of positive prescription. See below.

was conveyed to Tesco, thus inducing first registration. At this point the problem began to emerge. Tesco noticed the potential overlap of the titles and began negotiations with the Keeper to ensure that the disputed area was included in their own title sheet. At the same time Safeway had discovered, to their surprise, that their southern boundary extended further than they had previously thought. This was of considerable commercial importance. Safeway were to build a supermarket. A condition of planning permission was that they would construct a new bridge over the river. As the title had originally stood, only an expensive and awkward curved bridge would have been possible. The revised boundaries allowed a straight bridge.

At one level at least, the resulting legal dispute was relatively straightforward. When Safeway's title was registered on 8 October 1997 the disputed strip was included in the title plan. Hence, as a matter of law, Safeway became owners of that strip.[1] But since the inclusion of the strip was the result of administrative error, the Register was inaccurate and could, in principle, be rectified.[2] Tesco therefore applied for rectification. At this point they came up against the familiar problem of the proprietor in possession. As a general rule, rectification cannot be carried out where it is to the prejudice of a proprietor in possession.[3] Safeway were 'proprietors', at least in the formal sense that they were entered on the Land Register as owners of the strip.[4] Rectification would deprive them of ownership and hence be to their 'prejudice'.[5] The only question remaining was whether they could be treated as being in 'possession'. It was on this issue that the case largely turned.

It is difficult to possess a river bed but Tesco did their best. On 7 August 1998 Tesco had marker posts placed on the bed, including two in the disputed

---

1 Land Registration (Scotland) Act 1979, s 3(1)(a).
2 Actually it is possible to argue that it was not inaccurate in the hands of Safeway. When the alteration was first made, the Register was certainly inaccurate. But Safeway did not own at that time. Safeway acquired the property subsequently, from a person who, on the face of the Register, was owner of the disputed area. If it is accepted that the initial alteration of the Register had the effect of conferring ownership (an issue discussed below), it would follow that Safeway took the title from the then owner, under a disposition which expressly included the disputed area. What is wrong with such a disposition, and why should it be an inaccuracy to give effect to its terms? This argument amounts to saying that an inaccuracy can affect only the first owner and not successors. This argument is plausible or even persuasive. But in what follows we shall nevertheless proceed on the assumption that the Safeway title was inaccurate.
3 1979 Act, s 9(3)(a). There are, of course, exceptions but none was applicable on the particular facts. In particular the inaccuracy could not be said to have been caused by Safeway's fraud or carelessness (s 9(3)(a)(iii)). There was no question of fraud. It was not 'careless' of Safeway to fail to inform themselves as to the southern boundary; and even if they had so informed themselves it would not have been 'careless' to rely on the title plan on the Register: see *Dougbar Properties Ltd v Keeper of the Registers of Scotland* 1999 SC 513. Finally, and in any event, the inaccuracy was not 'caused' by Safeway but by the Keeper.
4 2001 SLT (Lands Tr) 23 at 34.
5 2001 SLT (Lands Tr) 23 at 37–38. The Tribunal was surely correct to reject (at p 38G–K) the argument that a proprietor is not prejudiced if he is able to claim indemnity. A person who otherwise falls within s 9(3)(a) is almost always in a position to claim indemnity, so that the effect of such a view would be largely to displace the protection for proprietors in possession. In fact the policy of the Act is that indemnity is always a second best and that the most deserving party should be given the title.

area. This was carried out using a crane supervised by an engineer in a boat. The poles carried notices which read 'Private property of Tesco Stores Ltd. Unauthorised access prohibited'. At this stage, the Lands Tribunal found, Tesco were not aware of the mistake in the title.[1] When the two crucial poles were washed away during the winter they were replaced, on 21 May 1999, with more robust posts which were placed on sandbags by divers. A month later Safeway removed these posts and re-positioned them on the part of the river which indisputably belonged to Tesco.[2] This 'tennis match' (in the phrase of counsel for Safeway) might have gone indefinitely. Instead the parties litigated.

If the facts did not disclose unequivocal possession by either party, that was more serious for Safeway than for Tesco. In order for Tesco's application for rectification to succeed it was not necessary to show that they possessed but merely that Safeway did not. It was argued strongly for Safeway that possession of part of a property must be treated as possession of the whole, at least where the boundaries were clear. By possessing other parts of the subjects registered under title number REN 56654 Safeway must be taken to have possessed up to the boundary as shown on the title plan. The Tribunal did not reject this argument out of hand. In some circumstances possession of a part might indeed be possession of the whole. But that depended on the size and nature of the unit. The property which happened to be encompassed within a particular title plan was often a matter of chance. The natural physical boundary was more important than a line on the plan. In the case of a river the natural physical boundary was the mid-point. Safeway's possession of other parts of the subjects could not therefore be taken to be possession of the riverbed lying beyond the *medium filum*.

Once the general doctrine was rejected it became necessary to show specific possessory acts. There was none other than the action, quite late in the day, to remove Tesco's poles. In the Tribunal's view this did not amount to possession of the disputed area. And since Safeway were not therefore proprietors in possession, rectification could proceed.

Rectification: from bad to just as bad

So far so straightforward. But the argument presented so far—indeed for the most part the argument of the case itself—takes no account of two awkward facts. One, considered later, is the fact that Tesco were also registered as owners of the disputed area. On the face of the Register the area was part not of one title sheet but of two; and both Safeway and Tesco were owners. The other, which requires more immediate attention, is the fact that Tesco's title was itself radically bad. Taken together, these facts create a legal problem which, under the 1979 Act, is more or less insoluble.

---

1 2001 SLT (Lands Tr) 23 at p 28C. Had they been aware, the Tribunal's view was that the possession might have had less weight.
2 These oscillating possessory acts bring to mind the various changes of locks in *Kaur* v *Singh* 1999 SC 180.

First, Tesco's title. Tesco acquired their property, lying to the south of the river, from J & P Coats (UK) Ltd in 1997. Coats' own title was an *a non domino* disposition of a few months before. Neither Coats nor Tesco were owners. Instead, the whole subjects, including the disputed area, belonged to some unknown third party. When, therefore, the disputed area was mistakenly included within Safeway's title at around the same time, the loss fell, not on Coats or on Tesco, but on the third party. Safeway did not take Tesco's land, for the simple reason that it was never the property of Tesco.

In *Kaur v Singh* Lord President Rodger referred to the person seeking rectification as having '*ex hypothesi* . . . a "better" title to the land than the proprietor whose name appears on the register'.[1] In the present case, however, Tesco did not have a better title. On the contrary, the title of Tesco was null and void. If any application for rectification was to be made, it should have been made by the 'true owner'—by the unknown third party—and not by Tesco.

The issue goes deeper than title to sue. Section 9(1) empowers the Keeper to 'rectify any inaccuracy in the register'. To allow Tesco's application is to say that the Keeper can rectify one inaccuracy by replacing it with another. The Register is not then improved. It is no more accurate than before. It is just that the mistake is a different one. Things have gone from bad to just as bad.[2] Nor need matters finish here. Since the Register is still inaccurate it remains vulnerable to further rectification. If Tesco can rectify Safeway's title, cannot Safeway then reclaim the disputed area by rectifying Tesco's title? Tennis match possession could be followed by tennis match rectification.

This is not to argue that s 9(1) could not be interpreted in such a way. Plainly it could. And the fact that the Keeper is empowered to make the Register inaccurate by *registration*—and does so every time he accepts an *a non domino* title—may support the view that the same can be done by means of rectification. But there is an obvious practical difficulty. A title is either good or it is not good; and rectification usually proceeds on the basis that the title on the Register is not good and the title of the challenger good.[3] So by rectification virtue is given its reward. But in a case such as the present, *both* titles are bad, and neither party is (in this sense) virtuous. How then is the Keeper to choose between them?[4] On what basis is one bad title to be preferred over another? It would be difficult to make a choice that was not arbitrary. If both titles are registered, one approach might be to favour the earliest on the register. In the present case, Tesco's line of title first appeared, in the Register of Sasines, on 11 August 1997. The disputed area first appeared on the Land Register in Safeway's line of title at some

---

1 1999 SC 180 at 194A.
2 Or perhaps even from good to bad, since, as noted above, it is not clear that there was any inaccuracy in Safeway's title.
3 Here, as always with registration of title, it is necessary to be careful with language. A title, once it is registered, can never be bad in the sense of being invalid. For by s 3(1)(a) registration by itself cures prior defects of title. When a title is said to be 'bad' in the context of rectification what is meant, therefore, is not that it is invalid but that it would be invalid but for s 3(1)(a).
4 He has a choice. Section 9(1) says that he 'may' rectify.

unknown date in July or August 1997.[1] There is no basis here for the application of priority based on time. A slightly more promising approach would be to give preference to the title already on the Land Register. All things being equal, there is something to be said for the *status quo*, and the title on the Register has at least the advantage of the technical validity which results from the act of registration. But that is no more than another way of saying that rectification will not be allowed.

Registration twice over

Title to the disputed area was registered in the Land Register not once but twice. First it was registered on 8 October 1997 in the name of Safeway under title number REN 56654; and then it was registered again in September 1998 in the name of Tesco under title number REN 93746. The idea that the same property can be registered under two different title sheets (other than by inadvertence) is difficult to grasp. Normally, of course, it would not occur. Initially indeed the disputed area was not included under REN 93746 but it was added a few months later following representations by Tesco. A practical justification is that it allowed prescription to run.[2] But whatever the justification, the result was to move into unchartered waters.[3] If the same land is registered under two separate titles, where does ownership lie? On the face of the Register the land belonged to Safeway, and at the same time and quite separately it belonged also to Tesco. It is true that the Tesco title contained the following, rather curious, notice:

> As regards the part tinted blue on the Title Plan [ie the disputed area], Indemnity is excluded in terms of Section 12(2) of the Land Registration (Scotland) Act 1979 in respect that the said part tinted blue was registered under Title Number REN 56654 on 8 October 1997 and ranks prior to the Disposition to Tesco Stores Limited registered 14 May 1998 on which the entitlement of the said Tesco Stores Limited was founded.[4]

But indemnity is not the same thing as title. The fact that title is not guaranteed has no bearing on its validity. Section 12 of the Act operates quite separately from s 3.

The notice did at least indicate the Keeper's view of matters. The owners were Safeway and not Tesco. The first to register were preferred to the second. And that view seems to have been accepted in the litigation.[5] Probably it is

---

1 2001 SLT (Lands Tr) 23 at 24K.
2 Indeed the Keeper's practice in this area, understandably enough, seems intended to reproduce the effect of the Sasine system. The grantee is given the opportunity of prescription, but until prescription has run he is not regarded as, properly speaking, the owner. The difficulty of course is that on registration a person *is* the owner, whatever the note excluding indemnity might say.
3 Note, however, that much the same issue arises if, following a conveyance *a non domino*, the Keeper enters the name of the disponee without at the same time removing the name of the previous owner. For a discussion, see G L Gretton and K G C Reid, *Conveyancing* (2nd edn, 1999) para 8.15.
4 In fact, since indemnity had already been excluded in respect of the whole title because its foundation was a deed granted *a non domino*, this was actually a double exclusion.
5 2001 SLT 23 at 25H and 37G.

incorrect. Admittedly the issue is one of considerable difficulty and only limited guidance can be found from the 1979 Act.[1] But the balance of argument strongly favours the view that the last to register—Tesco in this case—is the owner.[2]

To understand why it is necessary to examine once again the history of the title. Until 1997 the disputed area was the property of an unknown third party. The position changed when, on 8 October 1997, Safeway were registered as owners.[3] Here the effect of s 3(1)(a) of the 1979 Act is quite clear. Registration vests in the applicant 'a real right in and to the interest'; and this real right (in this case, of ownership) arises irrespective of the prior state of the title. Following registration, the Register might be inaccurate. There might be exclusion of indemnity. But the act of registration confers ownership on the person registered as proprietor. Safeway thus became owners on 8 October 1997. So matters remained until September 1998 and the registration in favour of Tesco.

Registration in favour of Tesco also triggered s 3(1)(a). On registration Tesco, equally, became owners of the disputed area. And because only one title of ownership is possible at any one time,[4] the fact that Tesco became owners meant that Safeway had ceased to be owners.[5] Section 3(1)(a), it will be noted, produces a single rather than a continuing effect. It made Safeway owners but it did not protect that ownership for the future. If someone else became owner—normally of course as a result of voluntary transfer by Safeway—then Safeway's own title would be lost.

The 1979 Act admits of one possible counter-argument. In terms of s 7(2) 'titles to registered interests in land shall rank according to the date of registration of those interests'. The word 'rank' here recalls the Keeper's note in excluding indemnity. The argument is simple. Rights rank in the order of registration; and since Safeway were the first to register, their title is to be preferred to that of Tesco. Almost certainly the argument is mistaken, for two reasons.

First, s 3(1)(a) is not qualified by s 7. This is not merely the technical argument that s 3 is not declared to be subject to s 7 (although that is true). It is that it would make no sense if it were. Section 3(1)(a) conferred on Tesco a real right of ownership. That is not a right which could 'rank' behind some other real right of ownership. Ownership is all or nothing. To say that one right of ownership 'ranks' behind another is to say the impossible. A second-ranking right of ownership—if the idea could be imagined—would be no right at all but a simple nullity. That result cannot be reconciled with s 3(1)(a).

Second, and more broadly, s 7 is about ranking and hence only about those real rights—most notably rights in security—which are capable of co-existing

1 One reason for this is that the idea of two concurrent registrations in the respect of the same property can hardly have been in the minds of those devising the scheme.
2 K G C Reid, *The Law of Property in Scotland* (1996) para 685.
3 For the possible argument that it changed earlier, in July/August 1997 when the title plan was changed, see below.
4 *Sharp* v *Thomson* 1995 SC 455 at 469F *per* Lord President Hope.
5 If A becomes owner of property owned by B, B must cease to be owner. So, for example, if A acquires ownership by positive prescription, B is no longer owner. In effect B has lost his ownership by positive (and not by negative) prescription.

within a hierarchy, that is to say which are capable, unlike the real right of ownership, of ranking.[1]

Earlier it was suggested that Tesco's application for rectification should have been rejected on the basis that the Keeper cannot be asked to replace one inaccuracy with another. The effect of the argument just advanced is to suggest that the application was in any case unnecessary. If Tesco were already owners, what did it matter that Safeway's title plan continued to show the disputed area? Any attempt by Safeway to use the disputed area could be met by interdict. Insofar as rectification was necessary, it was necessary only in respect in Tesco's own title, to the effect of striking out the Keeper's notice about indemnity. And rectification in respect of that notice was indeed ordered by the Lands Tribunal, though of course on different grounds.[2] However, it may be observed that if rectification had not happened, Safeway could have disponed to another party, who, having the most recent registration, would then have been owner, thereby ousting the Tesco title.

The end result is a direct consequence of the Keeper's decision, after representations, to include the disputed area in Tesco's title. He was under no obligation to do so. The Keeper can accept or refuse an *a non domino* title at will.[3] In accepting one in this case—and hence in triggering s 3(1)(a)—he was choosing Tesco over Safeway.[4] One bad title was being preferred to the other. With hindsight he should have gone further still and removed the disputed area from Safeway's title.[5] The position would then have been clear. As it is, anyone inspecting title number REN 56654 would assume, incorrectly, that the disputed area was the property of Safeway.[6]

Entering the Register

One other matter may be mentioned by way of a postscript. The 1979 Act provides a number of different ways in which material may enter the Register. Usually this occurs by registration under s 2, but other possibilities are rectification under s 9 and the noting of an overriding interest under s 6(4). There may also be a residual and continuing power to add material under s 6(1) although the provision is unclear.[7] The effect of each method is different. Registration, as we have seen, triggers s 3(1)(a) of the Act and confers real rights. In appropriate cases rectification appears also to have this effect although the

---

1 Cf K G C Reid, '*A Non Domino Conveyances* and the Land Register' 1991 *Juridical Review* 79.
2 2001 SLT (Lands Tr) 23 at 39B.
3 *Registration of Title Handbook* (2nd edn, 2000) para 6.4. The statutory basis is s 4(1) of the 1979 Act.
4 But apparently unknowingly if one is to judge by the wording of the exclusion of indemnity.
5 As he was entitled to do under s 5(1) of the 1979 Act ('and in each case by making such consequential amendments in the register as are necessary').
6 As indeed Safeway themselves so assumed, in reliance on the Register: see 2001 SLT (Lands Tr) 23 at 26I–K.
7 Section 6(1) is used as part of the normal registration process. But it is arguable that it also confers an independent power to enter material. This is suggested both by para (g) and by the opening words of the provision ('shall make up *and maintain* a title sheet').

Act is silent on the subject. By contrast, the noting of an overriding interest has no legal consequences, for by definition the interest is valid without registration and is not made more valid by being entered on the Register. Adding material under s 6(1), if competent at all, would seem to be similarly neutral in effect.

As this analysis shows, not everything that appears on the Register can be taken to confer rights. To some extent, it depends on how the material arrived. If, due to a computer virus, the names were to be changed in the proprietorship sections of 100,000 properties, there would be no change of ownership. This would not be registration, or rectification, or even an exercise of powers under s 6(1). It would be a technical error which could, and would, be corrected, preferably without telling anyone. The same would be true if a member of staff at Meadowbank House ran amok and made unauthorised alterations to the Register.

These remarks are prompted by the facts of the *Tesco* case, for on two occasions the Register was altered in a manner which is difficult to classify. One was when the title plan of REN 56654 was re-drawn following the digital conversion of the map base. The other was when, Tesco originally having been registered as owners of subjects which did not include the disputed area, the Keeper relented and added the disputed area to the title plan.

The second alteration can probably be classified as part of the registration process, even although several months elapsed between the initial registration and the alteration. If that is wrong, however, the addition of the disputed area would not then have the benefit of s 3(1)(a) and hence Tesco would not now be the owners.

The first alteration cannot, it is thought, be classified either as registration or as rectification.[1] If it is not to be discounted as merely a technical error, it must fall within such powers as the Keeper may have under s 6(1). Either way it could not act to confer ownership.[2] As it happened, the problem was short-lived. Within a few weeks the property had been conveyed to Safeway. In procuring registration Safeway procured ownership of the whole subjects included in the title plan of REN 56654.

SURVEYORS

Bank of Scotland v *Fuller Peiser*[3] and *Howes* v *Crombie*[4] were both cases in which the question was whether a professional person (a surveyor in the first case and a consulting engineer in the second) was liable to a third party (in the first case a lender and in the second case a subsequent owner) for alleged negligence. Both cases were decided by Lord Eassie and in both cases it was held that there was no liability. Both cases will be of considerable interest to conveyancers.

---

1 It could not be rectification because it was creating an inaccuracy and not removing one.
2 This issue is discussed, briefly, at 2001 SLT (Lands Tr) 23 at 31A–C and 34F–I.
3 2001 GWD 37–1411.
4 2001 GWD 28–873.

Once upon a time the law was that a person who made a negligent statement was not liable in delict to a third party who acted in reliance on that statement. For there to be liability for a negligent statement, the maker of the statement and the person relying on it had to be in a contractual relationship, or in the relationship of promissor and promissee. All that was changed in 1964 by *Hedley Byrne* v *Heller*,[1] which, though an English case, quickly gained acceptance in Scotland too. Since 1964 an important branch of the law of tort in England, and the law of delict in Scotland, has been exploring the consequences of *Hedley Byrne*.

In the *Fuller Peiser* case Mrs H P Mackay bought a hotel in Berwickshire, with the assistance of a loan from the Bank of Scotland, secured on the property. Before making her offer, Mrs Mackay commissioned Messrs Fuller Peiser to survey the hotel. That firm made the report available direct to the Bank of Scotland. However, the report was addressed to Mrs Mackay and contained the following disclaimer:

> This Report is provided for loan security purposes and for the use of the client only. It is confidential to the client and her professional advisers. The Valuer accepts responsibility to the client that the Report has been prepared with the skill, care and diligence reasonably expected of a competent Chartered Surveyor but accepts no responsibility whatsoever to any party other than the client. Any such party relies upon the Report at their own risk.

Later Mrs Mackay got into financial difficulties. The bank enforced its standard security, but the proceeds of sale were lower than expected, leaving the bank with a loss. The bank took the view that the survey had been negligent, and sued. Naturally the defenders founded on the disclaimer just quoted, and this defence was sustained. The fact that the report had been provided direct to the bank, and the fact that the report itself said (rather surprisingly) that it was 'for loan security purposes' were insufficient to negative the express and unambiguous disclaimer. This seems right: it has always been clear, since *Hedley Byrne* itself, that liability can be elided by a disclaimer.

In *Howes* v *Crombie*[2] George Fennell owned a property at Rosemarkie variously known as 'Butcher's Croft', 'Hill Croft', 'Viewmount', and 'Buachaille'. With his own hands he built a house there. Late in 1996 he sold the property to Jacqueline Howes. The offer sought the usual NHBC documentation, but the qualified acceptance deleted this and substituted:

> There is enclosed copy Planning Permission, copy correspondence re Building Warrant and Certificate of Completion and letter from Contract Services Building and Civil Engineering Consultancy dated 30 May 1996. No other documentation shall be delivered or exhibited.

The letter of 30 May 1996 was signed by Alan S Crombie, a chartered engineer, and was in these terms:

---

1 [1964] AC 465.
2 2001 SCLR 921.

> Having carried out stage inspections of the construction of the above property at Butcher's Croft from foundation to completion, I can confirm that the building has been structurally built using high quality materials and to a high standard of workmanship. The roof structure has been designed and supplied by Pasquill Building Components to current structural standards. I can certify therefore that the building is structurally sound and has been constructed using good structural practice.

The purchaser accepted this 'subject to confirmation from our clients' lenders that they find the documentation to be in order'.

The lenders were, however, not entirely happy with the terms of the letter of 30 May. This fact was communicated to the seller, at which point a further letter (addressed to Mr Fennell) was obtained from Mr Crombie, dated 28 January 1997, which ran:

> Having carried out periodic inspections of the house and garage constructed on Butcher's Croft, Rosemarkie, from foundation excavation to final completion, I can confirm the structural integrity of all the works and the quality of workmanship and materials throughout the construction and I am pleased to endorse the Local Authority Certification of the building works.

This proved acceptable and the transaction settled. Later, Mrs Howes discovered structural problems and raised an action seeking damages against Mr Crombie, alleging that the letter of 28 January 1997 had been negligent. The defender argued that even if the letter was negligent he was not liable to Mrs Howes, and the case was concerned only with that point. It was held that there was no liability. There seem to be two separate reasons for the decision.

The first reason was that there was no reliance. If one thing is reasonably clear in this difficult area of law, it is that the pursuer must show detrimental reliance. That is to say, the pursuer must show that had it not been for the existence of the negligent statement, s/he would never acted as s/he did. Of course, detrimental reliance in itself is not enough, but without it there can be no delictual liability for a negligent statement. The Lord Ordinary took the view that Mrs Howe had not in fact relied on the letter of 28 January. That letter may have been relied on by the lenders, but that was a different question.

It may be wondered why the pursuer did not seek to found on the letter of 30 May 1996, since there was a much stronger case for arguing that she had relied on that letter in concluding missives. The answer was disclosed during the case: 'Counsel for the pursuer ... volunteered ... that the pursuer could not found a claim on the May letter ... because it was issued at a time when no transaction respecting the property was pending and also because it was issued on the possible understanding that it would facilitate the issue of a local authority completion certificate.'

The second reason for the decision was that 'the pursuer has not demonstrated a relationship of such proximity that it would be fair and reasonable to hold that the defender, in writing the January letter, was under a duty of care towards the pursuer of the scope contended for by her'. Exactly why this conclusion was arrived at is perhaps not quite clear, but the Lord Ordinary seems to have approved the following line of reasoning by counsel for the defender:[1]

> Even if it were to be assumed that the defender did in fact have knowledge of the existence of an ongoing sales transaction, or that he ought to have appreciated that existence, it would equally be expected that the subjects would be independently surveyed by an intending purchaser, or by a lender whose survey report might commonly be communicated to the intending purchaser . . . It was not to be envisaged that anyone contemplating purchase or loan would place exclusive reliance on such an uninformative document as the January letter.

However the precise ratio of the case is to be analysed, the decision must be of considerable interest to conveyancers. Perhaps two points emerge. The first is that detrimental reliance may be impossible to establish unless the pursuer can show that, had it not been for the allegedly negligent statement, she would never have concluded missives (or made the loan or whatever). That is quite a stringent test. It is not a new test, but *Howes* illustrates it well. The second is that the statement will not generate even potential liability to third parties unless the maker of the statement could reasonably have expected a person in the position of the pursuer to see the statement and rely on it. That too is a difficult test to meet. And as the *Fuller Peiser* case shows, any disclaimers have to be taken seriously. The fact is that establishing liability to third parties for negligent statements, though not impossible, remains difficult.

JUDICIAL RECTIFICATION

Deeds sometimes contain mistakes. They may miss words out, for example, or use the wrong words. In cases like this all may not be lost, for in principle a deed with mistakes can be rectified by the court under s 8 of the Law Reform (Miscellaneous Provisions) (Scotland) Act 1985.[2] In recent years rectification has come to seem an increasingly powerful remedy.

Discrepancy between missives and disposition

The most straightforward case is where a disposition is in some respect inconsistent with the missives.[3] A court will readily be persuaded that the inconsistency was unintentional and that the disposition should be brought into line with the earlier agreement. The course of legal debate is helpfully described by Lord Macfadyen in *Renyana-Stahl Anstalt* v *MacGregor*.[4] There is an initial

---

1 Paragraph 47 of the transcript.
2 G L Gretton and K G C Reid, *Conveyancing* (2nd edn, 1999) Chap 17.
3 Thus *Cruickshank Botanic Gardens Trustees* v *Jamieson* 2001 GWD 19–735 (discussed below) *per* Lord Johnston at para 16: 'I consider this to be almost as clear a case for rectification as one can imagine against the background of the purpose of the 1985 legislation, namely to rectify mistakes based on a failure to implement a common intention'.
4 2001 SLT 1247 at 1257–8.

onus on the person seeking rectification to show that the disposition was intended to give effect to the missives. This is easily discharged, for usually the position is self-evident. Then it is for any person opposing rectification to show that, nonetheless, the particular discrepancy was intentional. For this purpose it is not enough that the person seeking rectification drew up or revised the disposition, or even that s/he signed it. A person may do all these things in error or without due attention.[1] Rather it must be shown that, somewhere between missives and disposition, the parties changed their minds, and that the discrepancy was intentional and not merely mistaken. There is no reported case in which this has been successfully done. Almost always, the discrepancy in the disposition is an obvious error for which rectification is an obvious solution.

One disposition

In *Renyana-Stahl Anstalt* the error was indeed, at the end of the day, found to be obvious. Missives of sale provided that the disposition should contain both an obligation on the sellers to reacquire the property in certain circumstances and also an obligation on the buyers to sell back in other circumstances. Only the first of these was included in the disposition. The sellers were successful in their application to have the disposition rectified to include the second obligation also.

A number of other issues arise out of the case. First, the clause in the disposition being imperfect as well as incomplete, the court allowed rectification in respect of imperfections as well as of omissions. The result, therefore, was a quite different clause. Indeed the improvements continued during the course of the hearing, for the sellers proposed further amendments and the Lord Ordinary added some of his own on the basis that[2]

> in light of the terms of s 8 ('in any manner that it may specify') it is open to me to make *ex proprio motu* those minor alterations, the possibility of which was discussed in the course of the debate.

Second, the missives were subject to a two-year non-supersession clause which had now expired. But the court rejected the view that this prevented the missives from being examined as evidence of the common intention of the parties. On the contrary, it was expressly stated in s 8(2) that regard may be had to *all* evidence.

Next there was an issue as to whether the two obligations were to be constituted in the disposition as personal obligations or as real burdens. The court's decision in favour of the former is reinforced by an argument which seems not to have been made. As the law currently stands, a disposition can impose real burdens only on the land which is being disponed.[3] This means that

---

1 Thus, Lord Macfadyen at p 1258E: 'The fact that the solicitors for the petitioners revised the disposition and approved its terms are as consistent with mistake or oversight on their part as with a change of mutual intention . . .'
2 2001 SLT 1247 at 1259G.
3 K G C Reid, *The Law of Property in Scotland* (1996) para 388. The position is liberalised by s 4 of the Title Conditions (Scotland) Bill (which is expected to be introduced to the Scottish Parliament during 2002).

while the second obligation (which was on the buyers) could have been imposed as a real burden, the first (which was on the sellers) could not. Curiously, in the unrectified disposition the first obligation was nonetheless declared to be a real burden.

Finally, the court decided that, since an application for rectification could be made either by petition or, in a case where other remedies are sought, by summons, an application (such as the one at issue) which was made by petition could not be accompanied by a declarator.[1]

Two dispositions

If the property has been sold on since the original mistake was made there will then be two dispositions to rectify and not one. In principle this is competent; but if the second purchaser bought in reliance on the terms of the unrectified first disposition, rectification of both will be prevented by s 9 of the 1985 Act (discussed below).[2]

There were two dispositions in *Cruickshank Botanic Gardens Trustees v Jamieson*.[3] The facts demonstrate the perils of relying on obscure descriptions in old deeds. The Trustees owned the Cruickshank Botanic Gardens in Old Aberdeen. In 1983 they sold number 8, The Chanonry, which is adjacent to the Gardens and was formerly the residence of the Professor of Botany at Aberdeen University. The disposition incorporated a description from an instrument of sasine of 1847. The house was sold on in 1990 when once again the 1847 description was used. Unfortunately, it was radically incorrect. Number 8 The Chanonry comprises around half an acre, whereas the 1847 description (expressed admittedly in Scots measure) extended to 2.5 acres and included not only the intended subjects of sale but also a substantial part of the Botanic Gardens including greenhouses and offices. The result of this error was that ownership of that part of the Botanic Gardens was duly conveyed, first to the 1983 purchasers and thereafter to the 1990 purchasers. Needless to say, the purchasers were unaware of their windfall and the University continued to manage the Botanic Gardens.

When the error came to light, the Trustees raised an action to rectify the two dispositions by having the Botanic Gardens excluded from the descriptions. The court readily agreed. The error in the dispositions was obvious and easily corrected. Evidence by the 1990 purchasers to the effect that they had thought they were purchasing more than the half an acre was rejected on grounds of credibility.

An unsatisfactory aspect of the 1985 Act is that the effect of rectification is generally retrospective, with the result that history is re-written.[4] Thus, the

---

1 2001 SLT 1247 at 1260–1.
2 Section 9 was perhaps overlooked by the Lord Ordinary when he suggested (at para 11 of the transcript) that, whatever the position of the 1990 purchasers, the 1983 disposition could be rectified if it did not properly implement the common intention of the parties to the 1983 transaction.
3 2001 GWD 19–735.
4 Law Reform (Miscellaneous Provisions) (Scotland) Act 1985, s 8(4), (5).

answer to the question, who owned the relevant part of the Botanic Gardens between 1983 and 2001, depends on when the question is asked. Until decree was pronounced in the litigation, the answer was the 1983 purchasers followed by the 1990 purchasers. After decree the answer was the Trustees. It is hard to believe that such casual reorganisation of the facts might not, in some cases, lead to strange and unjustifiable legal results.

Two specialities of the case were that the first disposition was granted before the passing of the 1985 Act, and that the petitioners (the Trustees) were not parties to the second deed and so were trying to rectify a deed in which they had played no part. Although the point was not argued, neither fact is a bar to rectification.[1] Indeed the interest of the Trustees to rectify the second deed was palpable, for only by rectification could ownership be reacquired.

The Trustees sought rectification of the second deed on the same basis as the first, ie that it failed to give effect to the common intention as evidenced by the relevant set of missives. They might have saved themselves some trouble if they had chosen to rely instead on s 8(3) of the 1985 Act. This provides that, where one deed is rectified, further deeds may also be rectified if they were 'defectively expressed by reason of a defect in the original document'. In other words, rectification will be granted if it can be shown (as surely it could have been) that the description in the 1990 disposition was simply copied from the description in the original break-off deed of 1983. There would then have been no need to investigate the intentions of the parties to the 1990 transaction.

In fact there was an even simpler answer to the whole question. It is settled law for Sasine titles that if A conveys to B but retains possession, the property, while initially passing to B, reverts to A at the end of 10 years.[2] The reason is positive prescription. Prescription requires both a *habile* title and 10 years of possession; but the original title held by A (ie the disposition in A's favour) is a sufficient title for this purpose. No application under s 8 was necessary, therefore, for the simple reason that the Trustees were already owners of the Botanic Gardens. Ownership had re-vested in 1993 on completion of 10 years possession.

Prejudicial reliance by third parties

Rectification is barred if it would adversely affect a third party who had relied on the deed in its unrectified form. The details are found in s 9 of the 1985 Act. In *Co-operative Wholesale Society Ltd* v *Ravenseft Properties Ltd*[3] s 9 was judicially considered almost for the first time. The facts are another unhappy tale. The Co-op were tenants of Ravenseft in respect of a unit in a shopping centre in Dundee. They reached an agreement that the keep-open obligations in the lease should

---

1 On the first point see *Bank of Scotland* v *Graham's Tr* 1992 SC 79. On the second, it has similarly been held that a third party to a deed can *oppose* an application for rectification if rectification would affect that party's position. See *Norwich Union Life Insurance Society* v *Tanap Investments VK Ltd (No 2)* 2000 SC 515, discussed in *Conveyancing 2000* p 120.
2 G L Gretton and K G C Reid, *Conveyancing* (2nd edn, 1999) para 7.12; D Johnston, *Prescription and Limitation* (1999) para 15.50.
3 2001 GWD 24–905.

be deleted and a minute of variation was entered into accordingly. But while this deleted the principal keep-trading clause of the lease, it overlooked clause 10.6 in terms of which the tenants obliged themselves:

> To keep the premises open for retail trade during the usual hours of business in the locality . . . the shop display windows being kept dressed in a suitable manner and in keeping with a good class shopping centre.

In due course Ravenseft sold their interest to Douglas Shelf Seven Ltd; and when the premises were not duly kept open in terms of clause 10.6 Douglas Shelf Seven Ltd raised an action of damages for £700,000. Faced with this claim the Co-op sought rectification of the minute of agreement to the effect of deleting clause 10.6 as (or so they argued) had always been the intention. Douglas Shelf Seven Ltd pled s 9. They had bought in reliance on the minute of agreement in its original form, ie so that clause 10.6 formed part of the lease. Rectification would be prejudicial to their position. At debate averments in support of this argument were held relevant and proof before answer allowed. Lord Macfayden's opinion, although only at a preliminary stage, contains a useful discussion of the meaning and scope of s 9.

PART V

TABLES

CUMULATIVE TABLE OF APPEALS 1999–2001

This lists all cases digested in *Conveyancing 1999* and *Conveyancing 2000* in respect of which an appeal was subsequently heard, and gives the result of the appeal.

Cheltenham & Gloucester plc v *Sun Alliance and London Insurance plc*
2001 SLT 347 (OH) (2000 Case (63)) *rev* 2001 SLT 1151 (IH) (2001 Case (73))

Conway v *Glasgow City Council*
1999 SCLR 248, 1999 Hous LR 20 (Sh Ct) *rev* 1999 SLT (Sh Ct) 102, 1999 SCLR 1058, 1999 Hous LR 67 (1999 Case (44)) *rev* 2001 SLT 1472, 2001 SCLR 546 (IH) (2001 Case (51))

Grampian Joint Police Board v *Pearson*
2000 SLT 90 (OH) (2000 Case (18)) *affd* 2001 SC 772, 2001 SLT 734 (IH) (2001 Case (17))

Inverness Seafield Co Ltd v *Mackintosh*
1999 GWD 31–1497 (OH) (1999 Case (19)) *rev* 2001 SC 406, 2001 SLT 118 (IH) (2000 Case (13))

Kaur v *Singh (No 2)*
1999 Hous LR 76, 2000 SCLR 187, 2000 SLT 1324 (OH) (1999 Case (34)) *affd* 2000 SLT 1323, 2000 SCLR 944 (IH) (2000 Case (26))

Minevco Ltd v *Barratt Southern Ltd*
1999 GWD 5–266 (OH) (1999 Case (41)) *affd* 2000 SLT 790 (IH) (2000 Case (36))

Robertson v *Fife Council*
2000 SLT 1226 (OH) (2000 Case (84)) *affd* 2001 SLT 708 (IH) (2001 Case (82))

Souter v *Kennedy*
23 July 1999, Perth Sheriff Court (unreported) (1999 Case (69)) *rev* 20 March 2001 (unreported) (IH) (2001 Case (81))

TABLE OF CASES DIGESTED IN 2000
BUT REPORTED IN 2001

A number of cases which were digested in *Conveyancing 2000* but were at that time unreported have been reported since. A number of other cases have been reported in an additional series of reports. For the convenience of those using the 2000 Volume all the cases in question are listed below, together with a complete list of citations.

A G E Ltd v *Kwik Save Stores Ltd and Brown*
2001 SLT 841 (OH)

Abbott v *Forest Hills Trossachs Club*
2001 SLT (Sh Ct) 155

Advocate General (for Commissioners of Customs & Excise) v *Zaoui*
2001 SC 448, 2001 SLT 201 (IH)

Ahmed v *Clydesdale Bank plc*
2001 SLT 423 (OH)

Burn's Tr v *Burns*
2001 SLT 1383 (OH)

Cheltenham & Gloucester plc v *Royal & Sun Alliance Insurance Co plc*
2001 SLT 347 (OH)
[The appeal in this case is noted in the previous table.]

Douglas v *Stuart Wyse Ogilvie Estates Ltd*
2001 SLT 689 (OH)

Elmford Ltd v *City of Glasgow Council (No 2)*
2001 SC 267, 2001 SLT 725 (OH)

Gardner v *Macneal*
2001 Hous LR 8 (IH)

Higgins v *North Lanarkshire Council*
2001 SLT (Lands Tr) 2

Knapdale (Nominees) Ltd v *Donald*
2000 SCLR 1013, 2001 SLT 617

Lock v *City of Edinburgh Council*
2001 SLT (Lands Tr) 19

MacKinnon v *Argyll and Bute Council*
2001 SLT 1275 (OH)

Maypark Properties Ltd v *Stirrat*
2001 SLT (Sh Ct) 171

Miller Homes Ltd v *Frame*
2001 SLT 459 (OH)

National Children's Home and Orphanage Trs v *Stirrat Park Hogg*
2001 SC 324, 2001 SLT 469 (OH)

Nottay's Tr v *Nottay*
2001 SLT 769 (OH)

Patterson v *Menzies*
2001 SCLR 266 (OH)

Sears Properties Netherlands BV v *Coal Pension Properties Ltd*
2000 SCLR 1002, 2001 SLT 761 (OH)

Stevenson-Hamilton's Exrs v *McStay (No 2)*
2001 SLT 694 (OH)